WHEN THE LAUGHING STOPPED

D1523143

WHEN THE LAUGHING STOPPED

THE STRANGE, SAD DEATH OF WILL ROGERS

JOHN EVANGELIST WALSH

UNIVERSITY OF ALASKA PRESS

FAIRBANKS, ALASKA

© 2008 University of Alaska Press
All rights reserved
University of Alaska Press
P.O. Box 756240
Fairbanks, AK 99775-6240

ISBN 978-1-60223-029-3 (cloth)
978-1-60223-041-5 (paper)

Library of Congress Cataloging-in-Publication Data
Walsh, John Evangelist, 1927–
When the laughing stopped : the strange, sad death of Will Rogers /
John Evangelist Walsh.
p. cm.
Includes bibliographical references and index. ISBN 978-1-60223-041-5
(pbk. : alk. paper) 1. Rogers, Will, 1879–1935—Death and burial.
2. Entertainers—United States—Biography. 3. Humorists, American—
Biography. I. Title.
PN2287.R74W35 2008
792.7'028092—dc22
[B]
2008009923

Cover design by Dixon Jones, UAF Rasmuson Library Graphics
Interior design by Paula Elmes, ImageCraft

This publication was printed on acid-free paper that meets the minimum
requirements for ANSI / NISO Z39.48–1992 (R2002)
(Permanence of Paper for Printed Library Materials).

CONTENTS

DEDICATED
to the memory of

CLAIR OKPEAHA
1891–1973

The Eskimo hunter who was the
last to speak with Will Rogers,
and who brought news of
the crash to the world

ILLUSTRATIONS

PROLOGUE: THE LIGHT ON THE BRIDGE

Will Rogers and Wiley Post in Seattle, the day before
they began their Alaska flying odyssey. Eight days later
both were dead.

THIS WILL ONLY TAKE a minute. It's a personal memory but for those who know little of Will Rogers, I think it will help narrow the gap back to that tragic day in 1935.

Taking him off at the peak of his unmatched career, Rogers' death was perhaps the saddest in show business annals. But it was strange, too, and infinitely solemn, because of where it happened—the lonely wastes of Alaska bordering the Arctic Ocean—and how it happened—the crack-up of a small, private plane in a shallow lagoon on the frozen tundra before the startled eyes of one small Eskimo family, five children and their parents. The strangeness of the scene was aptly laid out by the United Press at that time. *Irony in Will's Death*, proclaimed one of the thousands of headlines reporting the event: "Will Rogers, accustomed to appearing before the most brilliant audiences in the world, came to his spectacular end before the eyes of a few fur-clad Eskimos who never have seen a theater. The man who entertained millions, a friend of presidents and kings, died in the presence of perhaps the only people in the world who had never heard of him as 'the world's greatest humorist.'"

Nor does the strangeness end there. Another victim of the tragedy, her young spirit permanently blighted, was Rogers' own daughter, the lovely blond, blue-eyed Mary. A promising actress fast attracting attention, on the day her father crashed to his death she was on stage acting in an aviation drama built around two fatal plane crashes. Though she tried hard to resume her stage career afterward, and was actually signed to a movie contract, she never recovered from the shock of that awful coincidence. That story, too, is told here for the first time.

I was a boy of seven years then, living in New York City on Manhattan's Upper West Side. Our apartment building was at 1810 Amsterdam Avenue, near the corner of 151st Street. A walk of two blocks west took you over to Riverside Drive where you could see the huge George Washington Bridge spanning the Hudson River, lofty steel towers rising on opposite shores. Now people are accustomed to the majestic sight, but then it was brand-new, the bridge having been completed and opened only a couple of years before.

At night along its roadway, and its smoothly dipping support cables, it showed rows of dotted lights on its two towers. But mostly it was an enormous, shadowy presence looming in the dark. One night my friends and I spotted something different, something arrestingly new. From the top of the far tower, the New Jersey one, a broad, brilliant beam of light was shooting skyward. Piercingly it cut through the upper darkness, slowly undulating back and forth . . . pointing south . . . shifting north . . . then south again . . . then north. . . . Searching for a plane in flight? we kids asked.

"That's for Will Rogers," one of the older boys corrected. "Yeah," said another, "and for Wiley Post too."

The name Will Rogers I had heard. I had even listened, though impatiently, to him on the radio when my parents turned his program on—at seven I couldn't follow the rambling talk that kept my mother and father laughing and nodding agreement. My preference was for the Lone Ranger and similar gripping fare. The name of Wiley Post I'd never heard, not that I could recall. Of course my father knew who he was.

"That's the man who was flying the plane when it crashed," he explained. "Post was the pilot. He was killed too."

The sensational story of the crash I'd overheard in the talk of my parents and other people. It all made little impression on my young mind until the night that Rogers' death became linked with that dramatic beacon.

"The new light on the bridge," continued my father, "that's in memory of those two, Rogers and Post. A memorial, it's called. When the light went on last week they had a big ceremony. The papers had a story about it."

Recently, half afraid my father would prove wrong, I looked it up. There it was, in the *New York Times* for December 1, 1935, page one of section two. *Beacon Dedicated to Rogers and Post*, ran the headline, and there were no fewer than five subheads. The ceremony was indeed a big one, held before a large crowd under the high curve of the New York tower of the bridge, with simultaneous radio broadcast. A band played, a company of National Guard troops marched in, several speeches were given by city and federal officials, and Mae Post, Wiley's widow, said a few quiet words of thanks for the honor done her husband. While a bugle sounded Taps, a huge flock of carrier pigeons was released, and at last came a roaring flyover of the bridge by a dozen Coast Guard planes in formation.

The powerful beacon, said the paper, "would be visible twelve times a minute to airmen for a distance, in clear weather, of sixty-four miles."

Just out of curiosity I looked up another paper, one all the way on the other side of the country, the *Oregonian*, published in Portland. Under a page-two headline, *High Air Beacon Honoring Rogers, Post, Is Dedicated*, it gave a shorter version of the *Times'* lengthy account.

My father also said something else that stuck in my mind (these are not his exact words but pretty close): "A memorial like that, I can see it for Rogers. For Post I'm not so sure. From what the papers say it looks like the accident was his fault. He knew the plane wasn't just right and he still flew it, took a chance. He didn't understand about flying in Alaska, either, but wouldn't listen to the warnings. Anyway, that's what the papers say."

Recently I looked that up too. Again my father was right. . . .

I had meant to explain at length about my reconstruction of scenes and episodes that have elsewhere been skimpily covered, but I'll leave that to the extensive notes at the rear in which I discuss and defend my interpretations. Here I'll be brief: in the narrative I blend what the documents *say* happened with what, according to careful analysis and common sense, *must* have, or probably, happened. As to the conversations, where quote marks are used the words have either been taken verbatim from the sources, or there is good information in the sources as to the thoughts expressed, if not the actual words. Conversations *without* quote marks are known to have occurred, but the sources lack specifics. The difference of course is technical and has no effect on the reading.

Everything else you need or perhaps would like to know about the loved and lamented Will Rogers and his last days and death, you will find in the narrative, along with what happened to the unfortunate Mary. In a way, I think, her fate was the saddest, strangest part of all.

THE STRANGE, SAD DEATH
OF WILL ROGERS

. . . the government, on account of what they thought was a physical affliction by the loss of one eye, dident want to give him a license. Now they got men lookin' an' offerin' a bonus to One-eyed Pilots. You see, the eye that he lost saw the bad weather an' the bad landin' fields, this one just sees the good . . .

Will Rogers on Wiley Post, 1931

1

THESE DAYS, whenever he drove home from the studio through the lovely, low Santa Monica hills, passing the tall, wooden gates of the Rogers estate, Clarence Badger had a strong urge to stop and walk in unannounced. So far he'd resisted.

It was years since he and Will had last met, longer than that since they'd worked together on a movie. Ten or a dozen years at least. Will had been living in Beverly Hills then, not here in Pacific Palisades on this huge spread. To now, put off by the formidable, tight-shut gates, more than a little intimidated by Will's skyrocketing celebrity, after a quick glance, he'd just driven on by.

It was 1935, and the Will Rogers he knew all those years back, when they were both just getting into pictures—silents, then—with the popular but untried Will as star, himself as director, was different. Will was a name even then, of course, even before pictures, a headliner in vaudeville and on the stage, especially in the Ziegfeld Follies, where his roping skills and his chatty, slyly humorous monologues brought him national fame. Now he was a full-fledged entertainment personality, one of the biggest in Hollywood, one of the biggest anywhere, really unique. Leading movie star, popular author and newspaper columnist, favorite radio voice, a hit on phonograph records, sought-after lecturer, much-quoted humorous philosopher on life and politics, intimate friend of the great, including kings, prime ministers, and presidents.

With a man like that you didn't just drop in.

Only a year before, the movie magazines had listed Rogers as Hollywood's top box-office draw for 1934, beating out such luminaries as Clark Gable, Shirley Temple, Joan Crawford, and all the others. He'd reached that lofty rung on the strength of three pictures released that year, all talkies: *David Harum*, *Handy Andy*, and *Judge Priest*. The last, in which he played a foxy small-town judge, was his best so far, all agreed. Of course that homey, drawling way of his, that country charm was what shot him to the top. Even President Franklin D. Roosevelt wrote him a fan letter.

The year before that, 1933, he'd scored a smash hit in *State Fair*, opposite Janet Gaynor, and with two lesser outings had still captured the number two spot in the box-office rankings, behind Marie Dressier but ahead of Jean Harlow and Gable.

As if that wasn't enough, no one could match him for readership and influence as a newspaper columnist, with nearly seven hundred papers carrying his daily and weekly ramblings on everything under the sun. Add to that his popular records, best-selling books, and top-rated radio show, and you get some idea of just how big was the reputation of the Oklahoma cowboy (in whose veins also ran Cherokee Indian blood, he'd remind you). Of course, it all came from that one remarkable talent, his unmatched genius as a *talker*, his ability to hold forth in wryly humorous fashion on almost any topic.

Another Mark Twain, they hailed him, and his impact was much increased by his main focus: current events, people in the news, and up-to-the-minute issues and concerns. (Of course, that focus was also the very reason why, after his generation was gone, his fame declined, though much of what he produced still can make you laugh and think.) "All I know is what I read in the papers," was his well-known signature statement, the catchy way he'd begin many of his columns and ad-lib monologues. "I never met a man I didn't like," was another of his sayings, one which told you more about Will himself than the people he met.

Even with his limited vocabulary and fractured grammar he could still hit his target dead center in a way that no learned tongue could match, combining fun and laughter with rare insight and unusual common sense. He was a larger-than-life version of those witty hometown sages celebrated by Emerson, those "rude poets of the tavern hearth," who squandered their "unquoted mirth."

which keeps the ground, and never soars,
while Jake retorts, and Reuben roars,
Scoff of yeoman strong and stark,
goes like bullet to its mark . . .

Of course, Rogers carried the language "which keeps the ground, and never soars" to a perfection not often equaled by other tavern wits. Only that "un-quoted mirth" is off the mark. Few public men have been so often and so widely quoted as Will, called by many "the cowboy philosopher."

To make Will Rogers—talker, thinker, cowhand, roping artist, movie star, neighborly rebel, homespun sage, and professional funny man—you could say that God combined Mark Twain, Buffalo Bill, and Mr. Dooley, with a touch of P. T. Barnum and Peck's Bad Boy. "He sent the poor man away from the theater happy with simple, homey things," wrote one observer at his death, and he made the rich man remember the joy of simple things: "a wealthy man himself, Rogers managed through the brilliance of his technique to create the illusion of complete lack of wealth. No matter how many times he was photographed on his private polo field with his beautiful horses, the world always thought of him as a shirt-sleeved philosopher who stood on the front stoop and reviewed the world-parade in homely language."

No, you didn't just drop in on a man like that, not even if you found the gates to his huge estate invitingly open, which so far as Badger had seen during the past six or so weeks, was never the case.

Then came a day in midsummer 1935—the next-to-last day of July, as Badger recalled—when he found the gate standing open. He'd driven past it a ways before he braked to a stop. For a moment he sat still, thinking, then he backed up. "I shot the car through the gate's welcoming arms," he recalled years later, "sped along an ever-rising dirt road that wound its way through holly and sycamores, crossed sylvan devils, and came out atop a high mesa," where he halted to take in the spectacular view. The Rogers' back yard, he saw, was a wide expanse of the Pacific Ocean. His memory of his encounter that day with his old friend makes a fetching portrait.

A little off to his right, as he described it, stood an atmospheric, hacienda-type main residence and other buildings. Nearby, enclosed by a white fence, was spread a large field, a polo field, thought Badger. In its center "a lone figure was galloping about," swinging a polo mallet, evidently teaching the technique of the game to his mount:

> My first glance identified him. It was Rogers. I knew that he identified me, too, for as I climbed from the car I heard a shout, "Clarence!" then a sound of approaching hoofbeats. He leaped from his pony, vaulted the fence, and grasped my hand. "Howdy, Clarence," he panted, "gosh, been a long time."

"Hello, Will, how've you been?" said Badger. Adding with a smile of approval, "You've got a swell place here, wonderful. How is the family?"

Family was fine, all fine, replied Rogers. Both sons all grown up now. His daughter, Mary, too, and right then she was back east trying her hand at acting, doin' summer stock up in Maine. "But what're we standin' here fer? Come on up to the house. Let's hand Betty a surprise. Golly she'll be glad to see you."

Soon they were all settled with drinks on the sumptuous back patio, "with its little sparkling fountain and gorgeous view." Sitting round were the much-pleased Badger, Will's charming wife, Betty, who had indeed been glad to see him and said so, the two Rogers sons, Will Jr. and Jim, and the irrepressible Will, still just as talkative in private as in public, his old self.

"Here we spent an hour or so reminiscing," remembered Badger, "and it was a treasured, never-forgotten hour," not least because it was to prove the last time he would ever see his old friend. In a short two weeks Rogers will be dead.

The first meeting of the two had taken place some sixteen years before, on the Goldwyn lot in the summer of 1919. Rogers was about to do his second picture for Goldwyn, and Badger had been picked to direct it. He was climbing an outdoor stairway to his little office when, as he said, he first encountered Rogers "perched slouchingly on the guard railing" talking with several men dressed as cowboys.

"As I mounted the stairs I saw one of them nudge Will and casually flick his head in my direction. Will slowly twisted around on the rail and from under his Stetson shot me a quick, seemingly indifferent look. . . . I can still feel those appraising, analytical glances streaming down at me from under the brim of

Franklin Roosevelt and son James break up at a Rogers quip: "I don't belong to any organized political party. I'm a Democrat."

Will with his three children: Will, Jr., Mary, Jim.

Will stars in the Ziegfeld Follies.

Will and wife Betty.

his hat . . . his thoughts at that moment were easy to guess, so much was at stake for him. It was vital he have a director who could appreciate his unique talents and present them to their fullest value on the screen. As we shook hands I warmed up to him immediately."

Eventually, until Rogers decided to quit pictures and return to the New York stage, the two made fifteen silent films together, all quite profitable. Then when the talkies started up, Rogers came back to Hollywood, scoring an even bigger hit than he had as a silent star. This time he was under contract to 20th Century Fox, so Badger had no chance to direct him. But he was kept busy and in the space of only six years he was seen in almost twenty pictures, all of them big moneymakers. Two weeks before Badger's visit, his latest, *Doubting Thomas*, had been released and was running to large audiences and sparkling notices.

"Clarence!" suddenly volunteered Rogers. "Know who sent me a fan letter? Roosevelt!"

"No! What movie?"

"Last year after he'd seen *Judge Priest*. Betty, where'd you put that letter from Roosevelt?" he asked, getting up.

"I knew you'd bring *that* up," she said, taking up a book from the table at her elbow and pulling from it a folded sheet of paper. "It's on White House stationery and is marked personal. The date is October 8, 1934. 'Dear Will,' it starts." Betty read aloud:

> We saw "Judge Priest" last night. It is a thoroughly good job and the Civil War pictures are very true to life as I remember the battles of that period! Also, I am very glad to see that you took my advice in regard to your leading lady—this time you have one who is good to look at and can also act.
>
> I suppose the next thing you will be doing is making application for an appointment on the Federal bench. I might take you up on that!

"Will plays a judge in the picture," explained Betty, handing the letter to Badger, "which explains the joke about the federal bench. Since the picture was such a hit Fox is talking about making a sequel. But that can't be till next spring. Will's commitment for this year is done, he's made his three pictures."

Yeah, added Rogers, just the week before he'd completed his third film, called *Steamboat Round the Bend*, to be released in December for the Christmas trade. Another picture he'd finished before *Steamboat* would come out in October, *In Old Kentucky*. They'd kept him busy, all right, but now for the rest of 1935 he'd be free of the movie business and on his own!

"Tell you a secret, Clarence. I'm plannin' to leave these here parts next week. Goin' on a roamin' around holiday. Flyin' around, I mean. Me an' Wiley Post, we're headin' up Alaska way. Goin' to see Alaska!"

"That sounds great, Will, really great. Alaska! And with Post! How'd you get hooked up with him?"

"Me an' Wiley been friends more'n ten years. He's a Oklahoma boy too, y'know. He's been up there before, stopped in Alaska on that round-the-world flight of his. Had a little crack-up on the Yukon River, a sorta forced landin', nuthin' much. Made it to New York an' set that record."

"What'll you do in Alaska besides look around? Some fishing? Maybe some hunting?"

"No, nuthin' special, just wander around. I'd like to see that goldminin' town Skagway, and the old gold fields of '98, an' that Matanuska Valley where they settled all them farmers broke from the Depression. Maybe go all the way up north to the top, to that Barrow. Last human settlement on the continent, they call it. I've always been crazy to go an' see what it's like up there."

Betty laughed. "Will'd rather go traveling than sit at home any day. Practically went around the world by ship before he was twenty. Alaska's been on his mind I don't know how long."

"You ever drive around in a car on a Sunday," asked Will, "not knowin' or carin' where you went? That's me an' Wiley in Alaska!"

"I suppose you'll write about it?"

Smiling, Rogers admitted that his newspaper column was a good part of his reason for the trip. He liked traveling, as Betty said, especially by air—never could get enough of flying, though he didn't know the first thing about airplanes—and he really was crazy to see Alaska. But having just finished his third picture in a row he'd been looking forward to lazy days at "the ranch," as he called the estate. He'd decided to go when Wiley invited him, partly because it would provide material to write about. Sitting comfortably at home wasn't the best way to get ideas for his columns and other commitments. When he got back he'd still have his fall radio show to get ready, but he'd have plenty of time for that—several weeks!

When Badger's visit ended and he left, Rogers strolled with him down to his car. Later, Badger said he was able to recall almost exactly Will's last words that day: "After I'm back, Clarence, I'll get in touch with you an' the missus, an' we'll have us a real nice evenin' together, a good old pow-wow an' dinner with all the fixins."

2

BETTY AND WILL were up early the Sunday he left to join Wiley Post in Seattle. His flight from Los Angeles wasn't until late that night, eleven o'clock, so they'd decided to fill the day with activity.

Usually on Will's holiday jaunts Betty went along. This time neither one felt that she'd enjoy knocking around in a small plane, always cold, and spending some nights in a tent or a sleeping bag if they landed for hunting or fishing or to get a close-up view of whales or bears or caribou. There was another reason she didn't go, and it concerned the real truth about the flight. It wasn't only for pleasure, not for Post, and maybe not for Rogers either. Its actual, practical purpose was Post's hope and plan to explore and map out a new mail-and-passenger route to Asia, Russia in particular, by way of the Bering Strait and Siberia. Such a route would avoid a long flight over the Pacific—difficult and dangerous at best, and scary for the traveling public just getting used to air transport—an idea, as Post was well aware, that had great interest for a number of commercial airlines. If he could be the one to pioneer it, set it up, Post's own future would be assured.

Rogers wasn't certain that he cared or had the time to go that distance. So far he'd agreed only to the Alaska segment, seen as a leisurely vacation, a two-or-three-week delay in the Russian flight. For both this part of the trip and for the longer Siberian journey Rogers was paying all expenses (fuel mostly, and service and modifications to the plane, as well as food and other supplies, accommodations, and incidentals). The agreement was that he'd make up his mind about Siberia as they went along. If he decided to go on with Post, then Betty would cross to Europe by boat and meet him somewhere.

It wasn't a trip she looked forward to, she later admitted. She would have preferred that they both go up to Maine to be with their daughter, who was with a summer stock company at Skowhegan. A pretty blond whom everyone agreed had loads of talent, at twenty-two Mary Rogers was stagestruck. At the famous Lakewood Theater, for three months she would be kept busy learning her trade, appearing in one play while rehearsing for another to go on the following week. For mid-August, when her father would start for Alaska, she had the female lead in a thrilling aviation drama that had been a hit on Broadway only months before, *Ceiling Zero*. Its fast-moving plot was all about daring pilots and the hazards of flying, dramatically emphasized by two deadly crashes. It was one of the many plays, books, and movies in the thirties feeding the public's fascination with the adventurous, rapidly developing field of air transport.

Having Rogers finance the little expedition across the top of the world was important to Post. His fame as a pioneer aviator had never brought him much financial reward, and without Rogers he could never have managed the difficult, dangerous, and certainly expensive flight from California to Moscow and beyond. Originally he had lined up the backing of a major commercial airline, or thought he had, but that had fizzled, and he'd then turned to his friend.

In truth, the distraction and delay of the extended Alaska interlude, to satisfy Rogers, annoyed Post considerably. He would have preferred aiming directly for his target in Asia, stopping in Alaska only for necessary refueling. But Rogers was paying the bills, so the decision was his, and in any case he still hadn't said if he'd be staying on for the Russian leg. The unsettled situation made Post—a silent, testy man to start with—nervous and impatient, though he was mostly able to hide it.

"We took a long ride over the ranch the Sunday morning before he left," wrote Betty, remembering her last hours with her husband, who talked about making new trails on the place and other things he wanted done. "Then we rode through the brush to a hidden trail that led down into the canyon, where Will had built a little log cabin, and we dismounted and went in. I remember Will was sorry that he hadn't had a chance to stay there. The little wood cookstove was up and even the bunks and mattresses were there. I tried to persuade him to postpone his trip for a few days. We'd take our bedrolls down and camp for the night, I told him. But he said, 'No, let's wait till I get back.'"

In the afternoon they went to watch a polo game at a neighbor's place, and then went back home where Will and a friend "penned the calves and roped until suppertime." At age fifty-six, and long after he'd given up trick roping as part of his act, Rogers' favorite pastime was still going into a corral with a bunch of cattle and a lariat, and lassoing the animals for hours on end. As a young man he'd been just about the world's best trick and fancy roper, a true artist. He hated to think of getting rusty, hated to think he was no longer, as his early billing proclaimed, The Cherokee Kid.

That evening the two drove into Los Angeles, where at Will's insistence they attended a rodeo at the Gilmore Stadium. They sat in the grandstand and Betty found herself thinking that there was something out of place about a rodeo held under floodlights: "I missed the sunshine and the hot smell of cattle." But her husband, she saw, didn't at all mind the setting and was enjoying himself hugely. Since his youth in the old Indian Territory days in Oklahoma when he'd taken part in them himself, "Will had never lost his delight in the rodeo contests—calf roping, bulldogging, and bronc riding." Sitting there,

> . . . in our box under the floodlights I watched him grin and wave to the contestants as they rode by on the tanbark. He knew most of the boys in the show and as the evening wore on the old-timers came over to shake hands with him. Someone gave him a little wood-and-paper puzzle and he toyed with it unconsciously throughout the evening. It was a mannerism I knew well, and which was so much a part of him. His restless hands could never stay still. . . .

Those "restless hands" point up a fact about Rogers not often recognized, the sharp contrast between his energetic inner self—intensely and continuously driven, both mentally and physically—and his outer demeanor—relaxed and self-possessed, as if nothing really mattered too much and it would all come out right in the end. Of course, that outer demeanor was his stock-in-trade and in both aspects he was marvelously authentic.

After the rodeo they stopped at a little lunch counter for a sandwich, and reached the airport less than an hour before flight time. Even late at night the airport waiting room was full, so they went outside. Then it was time to go, and they returned inside. Betty recalled: "We said goodby, and with his overcoat over his shoulder and a roll of newspapers under his arm he stepped aboard." The plane took off and as it nosed up, "I caught a fleeting glimpse of him through the window. He was smiling."

Close by the couple as they bade each other good-bye in the terminal stood two uniformed airline attendants. Both were well aware that the man with the coat on his shoulder was Will Rogers. When interviewed by reporters twelve days later they claimed that they could hear Betty talking, and that her last words were, "Don't go, Will. Please don't go." If Betty saw that little piece in the papers—she probably did since it showed up as an AP release in a lot of them—she never denied it, in fact said nothing.

At San Francisco the plane dropped down for a brief stop at the municipal airport, drawing several reporters eager for details of the Post-Rogers aerial odyssey. As usual when surrounded by newsmen, the loquacious Rogers gabbed away at length, while doing his best to discourage any further interest in his personal travels. On this holiday he hoped for a relaxed daily ramble, the chance to mix with ordinary people on simple terms of friendship. Talking to the reporters at the airport he began by denying everything. *Rogers Won't Fly to Russia*, announced the headline on the next day's AP story (the length and detail of the piece show how easily Rogers could earn sustained press attention on any occasion):

> Will Rogers will not accompany Wiley Post to Russia for the very good reason Wiley Post isn't going to Russia. Anyway that's what Rogers said yesterday just before he climbed into a Seattle-bound plane....

"Yeah, I'll probably see Wiley in Seattle if he ain't already took off for Alaska. He's got a lot of friends in Alaska, Wiley has, and it's my opinion that's where he'll stop. Some of you fellows just cooked up that story 'bout the Russian trip."

Hollywood's Number One Philosopher reached Mills Field by cab after flight time, but the plane was late. "I counted on that," he grinned while searching his pockets for baggage checks, $10 bills, and reminder notes. He explained he missed the airport bus because he was busy "writing a piece for the papers. All 'bout San Francisco an' the folks in it, an' the way the bridges are comin' along."

Plane departure was at hand. "Lands sakes, I forgot to buy some magazines. Gimme that one an' that one an' that one—no the one with the red cover—hey porter, put my typewriter on my seat, will yah. Got some more pieces to write."

As he started for the plane he kept up a rapid-fire comment. "Ethiopia? Why there's not much to say 'bout them. They're jes' waiting fer it to rain or to quit rainin', I fergit which. Tell you, though, that was an interestin' piece in the paper this mornin' 'bout the American Liberty League hoppin' on the President an' the New Deal. They been hollering from the first an' the best thing they can do is leave it to the people and the Supreme Court. Those ol' gents know what they're doin' and why they're doin' it. People got a lot more confidence in the Supreme Court than they do in a lot of politicians. . . .

"Nope, no pictures, not unless you get that pretty stewardess in it." The pretty stewardess with a show of reluctance got into it. With a broad grin and a wave of the hand he disappeared. . . .

Next evening Will called Betty from Seattle. Everything was fine, he said. He'd met Wiley and had seen the plane, and was helping to get things ready. Two days later, early on August 7, the phone at the ranch rang again. It was Will, saying that he had only a minute and that he and Wiley were about to take off for their first stop. It would be Ketchikan, just inside the Alaska border in that thin little strip of land down along the coast of Canada. It was a hop of some seven hundred miles, five or six hours flying time, about.

In Seattle a happy Rogers exits the little red plane after a trial flight.

On the photo at right he notes: "She is a Beaut aint it. This was when we was trying it out first with the pontoons."

She is a Beaut aint it. this was when we was trying it out first with the Pontoons.
Dad.

Betty wished him good luck, said have a wonderful time, gave him her love, and reminded him that she'd be flying east in a couple of days to be with Mary for the rest of her engagement at the Lakewood Theater. Probably they'd be there in Skowhegan through the remainder of August, she said. The play, *Ceiling Zero*, had opened at the Music Box on Broadway in April and had run for three months. Folks in the Skowhegan-Bangor area should like it too.

Seattle did not give Rogers his first sight of Wiley Post's plane. That had come some weeks before, in late June in a hangar in Burbank, a Los Angeles suburb, where he went now and again to see Wiley and watch the plane being worked over.

Post's first plane, the one that made him famous, the *Winnie Mae*, had been retired. In it he'd made his record-breaking 1933 solo flight around the world (a feat he'd first performed two years before that, in 1931, but with a navigator). He now had a newer plane, a secondhand Lockheed Orion. With the help of several mechanics he'd altered its design and reconstructed it to suit his own special needs. New wings; a new, heavier, three-bladed propeller; and a larger, more powerful engine were the major alterations made in Burbank. He had also installed another gas tank, holding thirty gallons, wedged in under the pilot's seat. That gave him a total of six separate tanks for a total of some 270 gallons. Consuming some 30 gallons an hour at a cruising speed of 125 mph, the plane had a range on one fill-up of more than 1,000 miles in clear weather. Higher speeds and bad weather drank up fuel at a much faster rate.

An unusual feature of the plane was the one-man cockpit, which could be entered either from the outside through a sliding hatch, or through the small, eight-windowed cabin (four windows on a side). It had no name, only a number: NR12283.

Rogers had already ridden in it once, in July on a weekend flight to the home of a friend in Albuquerque, and he liked it. At first its landing gear was wheels, but in Seattle Post had the wheels taken off and replaced by pontoons. For Alaska, it was said, pontoons were much more practical, and no experienced pilot disagreed. He'd be setting down on water, they pointed out, far more often than on land. In the Far North, lagoons and lakes, bodies of calm, open water suitable for landing, were much more numerous and accessible than airfields. Of course most of the lakes and lagoons weren't convenient to civilization, which was a drawback.

So pleased was Rogers with the appearance, style, and accommodations of Post's airplane that he featured it in a column, apparently written as he sat in the rear of the plane's cabin at the dock, watching as it was being gassed up.

> Well all I know is what little I see behind this old Lockheed's wings. Its Sirius wings, Lockheed body, three bladed pitch propeller, big Wasp engine . . . ship looks mighty pretty. It's a bright red with a few trimmings of white stripes. The pontoons are awful big looking things but Wiley says "None too big."
>
> There was an extra single seat ahead of a double seat. Wiley took it out, and there is left a world of space, as there is this comfortable double seat . . . He has got a rubber boat and a canoe paddle, some life vests or protectors . . . his gun case . . . his fishing rod . . . Oh yes, and two or three coils of rope (they are not mine) they are to tie the ship up and pull it up to the banks. That will be my job to get out first and tie the rope and then vault ashore and tie it in . . .
>
> Well they bout got the gas in. Wiley is getting nervous. I want to get this off and leave it before having to send it back from Alaska. I am anxious to get going too. I think we are going to have a great trip, see lots of country that not too many have seen. . . .

(Betty Rogers, even after twenty-seven years of marriage, was still curiously impressed by her husband's low-pressure, almost nonchalant approach to his many commitments, especially the writing of columns and articles. "No one ever wrote so much as a line for Will," she once defended him. "His material was entirely his own; he even did his own typing. Taking care of his mail was the most that was ever done for him. And he never missed a newspaper deadline, though it was seldom that his articles were filed at the telegraph office or dropped into the mail an hour too soon. . . . He carried a portable typewriter in the back of his car, and had the faculty of being able to do his work wherever he happened to be, and always waited until the last minute.")

Rogers' presence in Seattle, and his projected Alaska flight, had not escaped the city's newspapers. On his arrival at the downtown airport he was greeted by the mayor and several officials. He was then escorted to the Boeing Aircraft Corporation's plant to inspect their newest product, the bomber that would become known as the Flying Fortress of World War II, the B-17. "The world's greatest bombing plane," Rogers called it, adding, "if we don't want it Abyssinia does," a nod to the war then being forced on Ethiopia by Mussolini, an ugly situation receiving news coverage daily and causing much worry in European capitals.

When reporters asked him questions about Post's plane he laughingly admitted that he could tell them nothing of any interest, though he was known as one of aviation's greatest boosters. Ask Wiley, he'd say, explaining that with Post as the pilot he didn't ever have to bother himself about the plane. "He's a marvelous flyer."

Post, with his wife Mae, had flown into Seattle a couple of days before Rogers, and the plane was berthed on huge Lake Washington, some miles outside the city. On the morning of August 6, with Rogers aboard and a mob of spectators watching, Post took it up for its first tryout with the new pontoons. During more than a half hour he flew it back and forth over the elongated, fifty-mile-long lake, banking, diving, roaring skyward, landing and taking off, getting used to the feel of the two large floats. They did, he found, noticeably alter the ship's aerodynamics, in fact more than he'd expected. The difference wasn't at all critical, however, and he had soon learned to compensate. Just needed a bit more practice.

For the final liftoff that day Will was aboard, sitting in the cabin on the one remaining seat at the rear (all the other seats had been removed to make room for supplies). "He's sure a marvelous flyer," said Rogers to the crowding reporters as he stooped out through the little cabin door after landing. "I'll fly anywhere with him, if he'll take me along."

In the crowd at the lake were several men, pilots and mechanics, who knew something about the handling of floatplanes. Those pontoons, they politely commented to Post, seemed awful big for the little Orion, too long and heavy. No, Post assured them, the floats might look oversize with the plane sitting there on the water, but they were the right ones for a ship of that size, weight, and conformation. The pontoon maker in New York had checked and rechecked them, as had the installer in Seattle, an experienced outfit. Even the little flying he'd done with them so far was enough to teach him that they were OK. The increase in drag needed a slight control adjustment, that was all.

Later that day Rogers was a guest at Seattle's Olympic Riding Club where he played an hour or so of polo. That evening he was a guest at the dinner of the Washington Athletic Club, and gave an impromptu half-hour talk to an enthusiastic audience of several hundred members. That night in his room at the hotel he wrote another of his weekly articles, tapping it out two-fingered on his battered portable. It listed the supplies they'd be taking on the plane (rubber boat and paddles, life jackets, guns and fishing rods, blankets, rubber boots, extra clothes, a small tent, a tiny stove, eiderdown sleeping bags, boxes of canned food including several crates of chili, etc.). He'd never used a sleeping bag, he ended, and didn't care for the idea of spending a night in one: "You zip 'em up around you after you get in some ways. I always have trouble with zippers so I can see myself walking around in one of those things all day."

The weather in the Seattle area on the morning of August 7 was good, though reports had started coming in of ugly conditions farther up the line. Heavy rain, low-hanging clouds, and strong winds, especially around Ketchikan. Would the two adventurers, asked the reporters crowding the hotel lobby, be going that morning, or would they wait for the skies to clear up ahead? It wasn't that bad, replied Post somewhat irritably. When Mr. Rogers got back from phoning his wife they were going.

The time was just before ten a.m. at Lake Washington when the little red plane, watched by a milling mob of people and reporters, taxied to the lake's center, squared around, picked up speed to the sudden roar of the motor, and lifted off. As the plane rose higher, again knowledgeable watchers on the shore had a question. Post's takeoff had been very abrupt and steep, almost a jump or leap into the air. With a seaplane, said those who knew, you had to remember the drag and pull of the pontoons, so much bigger than wheels. Liftoff from the water has to be smoother, more gradual, not so sharply nose-up. But still, said others, Post had that big, powerful engine, which must have offered a temptation to get aloft quickly. With that engine, commented one man, "he could take off from a frog-pond!"

From the few flights Post had already made in the plane, he was aware that, precisely because of that powerful engine, it had a little too much weight forward of its center of gravity, making the plane a bit nose-heavy. It was this tendency to imbalance that the drag of the pontoons increased. But it wasn't serious, Post insisted, only a matter of a different touch on the controls easily learned. In the cabin Rogers and the supplies would be kept to the rear as ballast, like rocks dumped into the hull of a sailing ship to steady the rolling.

As they covered the first hundred miles or so over Puget Sound, Vancouver Island, and up along the rugged Canadian coast, the weather stayed mild, vindicating Post's instincts. Only as they neared Ketchikan after some hours of flying did the going begin to get rough. At last, coming abreast of the low-lying city on the shore of Tongass Narrows, Post dropped down, and as they sped along, barely a hundred feet above the restless harbor waters, Rogers peered out the rearmost cabin window on the right. Rapidly passing by was what he thought "a very pretty little city right along the water's edge."

Post, half turning in his seat, abruptly called out above the loud hum of the engine, "I think we'll keep going, Will. Weather's pretty foul around here. If it gets worse we'll be socked in for who knows how long. Two or three days, maybe. Juneau's only another couple of hours straight north. OK?"

"You're the boss," agreed Rogers, not showing the puzzlement, and the touch of annoyance, he felt at Post's sudden need to hurry along.

Rapidly the plane began to climb.

3

THE LITTLE CURVED DOOR of the cabin swung open at an angle and out popped a head wearing a hat. Its brim was turned down but it sat perched well back on the grayish brown hair, so that the broadly smiling face was easily seen.

He was in Alaska at last! thought Will Rogers as he looked up at Juneau's weathered, old-fashioned buildings lining the narrow, sloping streets under the towering bulk of the mountain behind them. It wasn't the huge main portion of the enormous state (about double the size of Texas), only the short panhandle strip down along the Canadian coast. But it was Alaska, in fact Alaska's capital.

From the crowd on the dock burst clapping and a welcoming cheer as a pair of shoulders emerged, followed by the rest of the crouching body. On the plane's broad, low wing Rogers straightened up, the smile widening and both hands waving his appreciation of the warm greeting.

The transparent hatch closing the plane's cockpit was shoved back, drawing the crowd's attention. In the cockpit Wiley Post stood up, also smiling and waving, and the applause sounded again. How so many people in Juneau had been alerted to their arrival was no mystery. Many simply saw the colorful red craft coming in and down, guessed who it was from the newspaper stories, and hurried to the dock. Others knew when the plane was due because word had been radioed up from Ketchikan some three hours previously when the plane failed to make its announced stop there. Post's estimate of another couple of hours had been nearly doubled by the increasingly bad weather.

On the dock there were more newspaper interviews, and friendly exchanges with the delighted crowd. Then Post was approached by a tall, moustached man who announced his presence by giving Post a slap on the shoulder. "Joe, you made it!" yelped Post, turning and extending his hand. "Hey, Will," he continued, pulling at Rogers' elbow, "here he is, Joe Crosson, the man who saved my bacon in '33!"

"Hello, Joe, glad to meetcha," said Rogers, taking Crosson's hand. "Wiley here tells me that you're the best pilot that Alaska ever had. Or ever will have."

"Yeah, but you know Wiley," laughed Crosson. "Ten years I've known him, and you should hear what he says to me about my flying when we're alone."

"He always says he owes you a lot for what you did on that flight of his in '33. He might still be sittin' there with his wrecked plane in the wilderness if you hadn't come up with a new propeller an' such an' gone out there with your mechanic. Never woulda been the first man to fly alone round the world. Never woulda set that record."

Crosson smiled and flicked a dismissive hand. He had a car with him, he said. If they were ready he'd take them to the hotel where he'd booked rooms, the Gastineau. Nice place, not fancy but comfortable.

The thirty-two-year-old Crosson, it seems, really *was* Alaska's best pilot, one of them, anyway, one of the few. Bush pilots, they were fondly called, though there weren't many bushes where they flew, often only thick, all-smothering fog and obscuring mists, piercing winds, deep-packed or swirling snow, and paralyzing ice covering a rugged terrain of mountains and glaciers. Extreme cold, and at certain times interminable darkness, completed the harrowing picture.

Crosson had been flying in Alaska now for nine years in just such impossible conditions, in flimsy planes performing remarkable feats—mercy missions to deliver medicines or emergency supplies, daring rescue attempts and searches for lost flyers and passengers. Only five years before had occurred his best-known accomplishment to then, when he led the long search for the lost flyer Carl Ben Eielson, and his navigator, Earl Borland. Called the Father of Alaskan aviation, Eielson had single-handedly pioneered the state's air age, only a few years back, and in his own time was far-famed. In 1929 on an emergency flight to supply an icebound sailing vessel off Siberia's northern coast, Eielson's plane disappeared. For weeks on end, piloting an old, open-cockpit biplane, Crosson led the search, and it was he who finally found the wrecked, half-buried Eielson plane. Nearby under two feet of snow lay the battered, frozen bodies of Eielson and Borland.

Crosson himself had several times looked death in the face, and had survived only because of his daring, endurance, flying skills, and knowledge of the Arctic. When he wasn't performing heroic deeds he was still mostly in the air, ferrying passengers and supplies to and from small, rough landing patches in remote gold fields, or to regular airports in towns and cities in Alaska, or "outside."

Less thrilling but still difficult and dangerous were such exploits as his being the first to fly over, and land on, cloud-piercing Mt. McKinley, determining its altitude as the highest peak in North America. Also well-covered by the newspapers was his part in the race to bring back movie film of the dirigible *Norge* flying over the North Pole. When Post and Rogers met him that August 1935 he was head pilot in Alaska for Pan American Airways, which had just bought up and consolidated several smaller Alaskan airlines (Pacific

Alaska Airways was the line Joe flew for). His home was in Fairbanks, almost Alaska's geographical center, more than a thousand miles to the northwest, where he'd left his wife and three children to come to Juneau for the meeting with Post and Rogers.

On the ride into town Crosson handed Rogers a book titled *Arctic Village*. Its author was an eastern tenderfoot named Robert Marshall, who'd been fascinated by the "Arctic frontier." For fifteen months in 1929 and 1930 he'd lived in a little place called Wiseman in the nearly primeval Koyukuk region north of Fairbanks (the size of Massachusetts and New York State combined, it had a white population of only 127). With charming simplicity the book told of life in the Koyukuk, for both Eskimo and white, and it promptly caught Rogers' attention. For the rest of his stay in Alaska he carried the book with him, finding a moment here and there to open it, especially during the long hours in the air.

Crosson also had a message for the two travelers. They were to be honored guests that evening at a banquet arranged by the state's governor. Afterward they'd be interviewed on the radio.

Post looked disgusted. Rogers shook his head and sighed. They'd been hoping to avoid such public involvement on the trip, especially now, having just completed a thousand-mile, eight-hour flight through mucky weather. But they accepted, and both events went off well. The banquet, held at the territorial mansion, was relaxed and the food was good (Alaska king crab and Alaska salmon). Afterward, the two with Crosson were driven to the radio station.

Post spoke first, saying that their plans for seeing Alaska were vague. "I've always had a good time here," he explained, "except when I broke down and got lost on my trip around the world, and even then there was a good friend—Joe Crosson, here—to come along and pull me out of it." Subduing his impatience at the thought of wasting so much time doing what seemed to him nothing, he finished, "We plan to sort of wander around in the interior and see a lot, and hunt and fish and just sort of wander around."

Rogers then came on, giving his listeners what he knew they wanted from him—meandering fun poked half seriously at stray items in the news. He didn't stay on long, five or six minutes, and ended with one of his trusty old sallies: "People wonder where I get all my jokes. I just listen to the government and report the facts. I have 96 senators working for me and all I do is write down what they say."

Juneau was an interesting little city, but hardly the Alaska that Rogers wanted so much to see, and the two hadn't meant to spend more than a night there. A hundred or so miles to the north lay the colorful old gold rush town of Skagway, so intimately linked to the mining excitement less than forty years before. Above Skagway rose the famous old Chilkoot Pass, rugged entrance to the Yukon through which had poured so many thousands of eager prospectors. Next morning, they expected, after refueling and servicing the plane, they would make the barely hour-long flight to Skagway, staying there for a couple or three days. Where they'd be going after that they had no clear idea, only that it would be to the northwest, skirting the Canada border and taking them over into Alaska proper, the huge state's frozen interior. Maybe they'd head straight for Anchorage from Skagway, a little hop of only five hundred miles, stay a few days, and then jump straight up for Fairbanks, only four hundred miles.

It was the weather that kept them in Juneau, a cloudburst of heavily dashing rain. They were in for a drenching, everyone said, but it wouldn't last too long. Probably by early next morning or next afternoon they'd be on their way.

Rogers spent the early hours of August 8 in his room at the hotel reading and enjoying *Arctic Village*, the book given him by Crosson, greatly stimulating his personal curiosity about Alaskan life. The Koyukukers enjoyed, wrote Marshall, "the happiest civilization" he'd ever encountered, and his account went far toward proving the claim.

Post went out to see about servicing the plane. Rogers put aside the book and went out to a store. He was recognized and people crowded round, giving him his next column: "Fellow comes up and says I see all your pictures. I ask him which ones and he can't name a one. Woman brings a little girl up and says Tillie wants to meet you, she reads all your little articles in the papers. Tillie says, 'Who is he, Ma?'"

When the go-getting Juneau Chamber of Commerce heard that Rogers was still in town it pleaded with him to speak at its monthly luncheon that

Rogers, Leonhard Seppala, famous Alaskan musher, Post, and Joe Crosson.

The Post plane in Fairbanks, Rogers on wing, Post in cockpit, Crosson in lower right corner.

afternoon. He went and delivered another rambling, laugh-filled talk on current events.

Unexpectedly that evening their busy stopover in Juneau was drawn out further still, when an old friend walked in on them as they sat at dinner with Joe Crosson in the hotel dining room. It was the popular novelist Rex Beach, whose novel *Laughing Bill Hyde* had supplied the script for Rogers' first silent movie in 1918. Settling down together, the four enjoyed hours of good talk and laughter until well after midnight when, as Beach recalled, "Wiley went to sleep at the table with his head on his arms."

Before they were finished that night they talked a lot about flying in Alaska, its peculiar dangers in passing over the rugged, frozen land, and the need for pilots willing to learn its special conditions. With that, recalled Beach, "Will told me that Wiley was the most careful pilot he had ever flown with, almost too careful, it seemed to Will."

Did they plan to go up to Barrow, asked Beach. It was a long flight, of course, if they went from Juneau or even from Seward, clear across the state from bottom to top, maybe fifteen hundred miles. Not much to see when you got there, either, only a little village of a few hundred Eskimos and a few whites. But then you could say you'd been to the top of the world, the very tip-top of the North American continent, its last human settlement on the way to the Pole.

Rogers said, yes, he'd heard about Barrow, and they had thought some about going up for a visit. They'd see. Wiley wasn't excited by the idea of a long flight to nowhere, but they'd see.

Making the distant location even more attractive for a visit, added Beach, was the chance to meet Charlie Brower. If Will was looking for interesting people to write about he shouldn't miss the legendary Brower, who had gone up there as a young man fifty years ago. Been adventuring there ever since, said Beach, even married an Eskimo and settled down with his dozen children. One of the few white men to go out whaling in those flimsy little boats with the Eskimos, things like that. Nobody knew more about life high up in the Arctic Circle, or about polar exploration. Knows, or knew, everyone from Amundsen and Stefansson to Sir Hubert Wilkins, and all the famous bush pilots, ship captains, and who-all. King of the Arctic, they call him.

Rogers' interest was obviously aroused by the mention of the colorful Brower. He said he'd like to hear more about the man sometime when he wasn't so sleepy. If he didn't get to bed soon he'd be snoozing on the table just like Wiley there.

Before noon next day, watched by several hundred eager spectators, the gassed-up seaplane was again standing in the wide bay, riding gently on the water at the dock. As Rogers and Post walked up, someone in the crowd shouted a question: "Where you going?" Turning, Rogers called out, "Goin' to Skagway. An' to that there Chilkoot Pass. S'long!" He waved, walked down three or four stairs, stepped onto a pontoon, climbed up on the wing, and ducked into the cabin through the little arched doorway. Post settled into the cockpit and pulled the transparent hatch shut over his head.

Engine gunning, the bright red plane taxied out to clear water, headed round into the wind, sped away into the uncluttered harbor, and took off, its pontoons lifting through "a smother of foam," as the newspapers expressed it the next day.

Back in the city, Joe Crosson started his own preparations for his return home to Fairbanks. With one of the Pan Am mechanics at the company hangar he had an exchange about something he'd noticed when the Post plane was being serviced, something that had surprised him. Of the six gas tanks, only one had a fuel gauge, the thirty-gallon tank under the pilot's seat. For the other five tanks—two in each wing with some sixty gallons each and a smaller one over the pilot's head—Wiley would have to keep track of the known supply, switching from tank to tank as needed. Most private plane owners liked it that way, and the experienced Wiley shouldn't have any trouble with it. Still, for Alaska, it wasn't the best way.

Crosson had also been surprised by Wiley's abrupt, nose-high takeoff—no wonder the sharply angled pontoons had whipped up "a smother of foam." He had enough engine to do it that way, no question, but with so much open room in the smooth, spacious harbor it was really unnecessary. He could, and should, have gone up at a much lower angle and with less power, the safe way, as all seaplane pilots did. But that was Wiley.

Well, decided Crosson, he'd be seeing them in Fairbanks in a few days. He'd mention the matter then.

At that moment the stubby red plane with the big yellow pontoons was still in the air, passing high over Skagway. But it was continuing on north, not dropping down for a landing at the famous old town. Again Post had talked Rogers into changing his destination. Now they were headed north for Dawson in the Canadian Yukon, another old gold rush town some four hundred miles farther on.

The plan was that after an overnight halt at Dawson they'd go not west into Alaska, but still farther north into Canada, to a little town on the Mackenzie River named Aklavik. The Russians had set up a temporary station there, partly for commercial purposes but mostly to help direct an imminent attempt by two Russian aviators to fly over the North Pole from Moscow to San Francisco. It was still another effort to link the hemispheres by air, not very different from Post's own design in the opposite direction. At Aklavik he'd have a chance to catch up on the Russian progress, matters such as their intended route, where they'd refuel and how often, and their schedules. Up-to-date information about conditions in Siberia and for the flight on to Moscow, he assured Rogers when suggesting that they skip Skagway, would be good to have, maybe vital.

STILL TODAY RUSTIC in feeling and appearance, the little village of Barrow sits isolated at the top of the world. For some months each year the sun never completely sets. Thick sheets and massive chunks of ice close it in on the north, and the lofty, jagged peaks of the Brooks Range shut away the rest of Alaska to the south.

Perched on the frozen shore, built around a half-mile-wide lagoon, it's the last place in America where you can get a cup of coffee before you're afloat on the trackless Arctic Ocean. To get that coffee today you can drop into any of several small cafés and restaurants. To get it in 1935, you would have had to call at the home of one of the four white families in residence. There were no cafés then, and in any case few of the village's several hundred Eskimos cared for coffee.

Of the four white families in Barrow's small American colony in 1935, three were there for professional reasons, not because they preferred life in the frozen north.

There was Dr. Henry Greist, aged sixty-eight, Presbyterian minister and licensed physician, and his wife, Mollie, a professional nurse. They had three grown children, all now pursuing their own lives "outside." By that August the Greists were just recovering from their labors in the serious flu epidemic that had swept northern Alaska in the spring (in the Barrow area there had been eighteen deaths, mostly Eskimos). The doctor's spare time, when he had any, was given to preparing a newsletter—writing, mimeographing, and mailing it out himself, giving news and comment on life in the Arctic. He called it *The Northern Cross*, and only occasionally slipped in a sermon or religious exhortation.

There was Frank Daugherty, aged forty-two, a teacher assigned to the distant post by the public school system, and his wife, Elizabeth. They had two young children, both living in Barrow with them. Daugherty also had charge of the village's Native affairs, and was reindeer commissioner for the Barrow area. Well read, idealistic, he was also "a genius with tools," and had built a playground for the schoolchildren, including a real merry-go-round. He was, all agreed, "the right man in the right place."

There was Stanley Morgan, aged thirty-four, a sergeant in the U.S. Signal Corps, with his wife, Beverly, and three children. As head of station, he kept his eye on things for the army, but his main role was as sole wireless-telegraph operator, in which he gave the isolated community its only means of fast communication with the outside world. The telephone, voice radio, and even electricity had yet to reach that far into the Arctic Circle (except for a small generator at the hospital). His spare time, when he had any—the simple details of life in the Arctic demanded lots more attention than did warmer climes—was given to photography, for which he'd fixed up a neat little darkroom.

Fourth was a tall, burly man who lived there because he would not live anywhere else, Charlie Brower. A youth of eighteen when he arrived in Barrow aboard a sailing vessel, he was now seventy-two. With him was his Eskimo wife, along with a horde of children, at least a dozen (he'd been married twice, both times to Eskimo women). Existing for long as an independent trader-trapper-hunter, and sometime whaleman on the seasonal commercial whalers that came up from the lower states, he was now living a much less strenuous life as a fur trader and animal and specimen collector for zoos, museums, and naturalists. He was also a consultant for archaeologists and Arctic expeditions. Recently he had accepted the post of U.S. Commissioner for Barrow and its surroundings, a government official combining mayor, police chief, school and health administrator, and general factotum. The honorary title bestowed on him in the occasional news stories about his exploits, "King of the Arctic," reflected the great variety of northern life he'd seen and experienced.

Also part of Barrow's white community was a mysterious elderly gentleman described as "an old Scotch whaleman." About him nothing further is known except that he hadn't spent a whole day away from Barrow since the 1890s and had never seen such wonders as automobiles and telephones. Many of Alaska's northern villages, it seemed, enjoyed the presence of at least one such intriguing character. They always generated rumors about why they were there and what their personal stories were. Barrow's mystery man bore the name A. H. Hopson, but that's all that's known of him.

Of the five men, Dr. Greist, tall and distinguished, was most important to the village, even aside from his ministerial capacity, for both whites and Eskimos. A dozen years earlier he and his wife had set up and now ran the community's hospital, a small building at the village center, the only medical facility for many miles around. Mollie Greist, besides supervising the tiny hospital and its staff of young Eskimo girls, had also begun a baby clinic where she taught the Eskimo women the latest in pregnancy and infant care.

At times overwhelmed by lack of staff and shortage of medicines, Greist also had to bear the insolence of government officials "because of a prejudice against the missionary doctor" as less than professional. After the flu epidemic had subsided in May a government doctor, ignorant of Eskimo life, had come up from Fairbanks "to check upon our efficiency generally and to ascertain why we were losing so many cases among our ill of influenza." After a quick, overnight inspection, the official offered some sharp observations on Barrow's medical procedures, then flew off, leaving behind a fuming Dr. Greist.

What such hurried government inspectors often failed to see and understand about men like Dr. Greist in the Far North was their value in addition to their assigned duties. Here is how "The Fourth of July in Barrow," in 1935, is described in the August *Northern Cross* newsletter, centered on the Eskimo families:

> The Fourth was celebrated in Barrow by games upon the beach, stunts, etc., for which prizes were offered by the whites and by the native store. A baseball game was had late, beginning at near midnight and ending at or near 2 A.M., the sun having shone brilliantly the while out over the frozen sea hard by . . .
>
> Mrs. Greist and her girls served a dinner, for the babies and their mothers, then for the old folks. She served boiled rice with milk a'plenty mixed therewith, crackers, tea, milk as a drink for the little tads, and allowed them all they could hold. The writer took pictures of them as they ate, at a low table of boards running the entire length of the long porch, every mother seated flat upon the floor, the kiddies old enough likewise also seated, all spooning in the grub ravenously. . . after the feast was finished, for all the kiddies there came popcorn, peanuts, and candy.
>
> The porch was decorated with American flags, and the walk between the manse and hospital was lined with tiny flags, stuck into the earth.

The Greists lived in a wooden frame house provided for them by the Presbyterian Mission Society. It had been designed by Greist himself and built with Eskimo help, and proved surprisingly comfortable: dining room, parlor, kitchen, bathroom, and two bedrooms upstairs. The floors had special insulation and all the rooms were airtight, with a unique arrangement of ducts for indirect ventilation. There was no furnace (needed too much fuel), so heat from the kitchen stove was sent up to the bedrooms through wall-and-ceiling registers, and each of the downstairs rooms had a woodstove of its own. One visitor described the Greists' little Arctic home as having "the authentic American flavor," no different from those "outside." On the windows, chintz curtains draped neatly open. On the walls hung engravings of

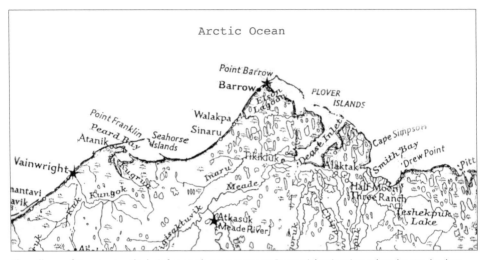

The village of Barrow on Alaska's far northern coast was Rogers' destination when he crashed at Walakpa. Home to several hundred Eskimos, Barrow had few whites.

Barrow today, much more built up. In the distance, looking southeast, still stretches the forbidding waste of the frozen tundra.

Charles Brower, of Barrow, as he looked in 1935 after adventuring for more than fifty years in the Far North. Known as "The King of the Arctic," Brower was the man Rogers wanted so much to meet and write about.

ACME NEWSPICTURES, INC. FROM O'BRIEN, WILL ROGERS, 1935

Acme Newspictures, Inc.

(top) The small Barrow hospital, the only medical facility for 500 miles.

(middle) Sergeant Stanley Morgan and son. Morgan's wireless telegraph was the only quick link between Barrow and the "outside."

(bottom) Medical missionary Rev. Henry Greist and his wife Mollie. He was the Barrow area's only doctor.

woodland scenes. A comfortable sofa was arrayed with bright pillows. On a windowsill a long, narrow planter held a mass of climbing nasturtium.

Morgan, Brower, and Daugherty, and presumably the old Scotch whaler, enjoyed comforts more or less similar, even when the snow piled high against the doors and icy winds blew. Brower's place was the most elaborate, his sturdy wooden house surrounded by an array of storage sheds and wooden racks for holding upturned boats when out of the water. A few Eskimos also had standard houses, but most preferred simple shacks, sod huts—the entrances outlined by a spread of whale ribs—or tents, and a few outlying igloos. Together the white and Eskimo dwellings in the village formed a spreading pattern dotting the tundra around a large, circular lagoon, the whole assemblage sitting just yards back from the bleak Arctic shore.

Animal life abounded in the area, particularly caribou, reindeer, seal, walrus, and whale, providing an endless supply of meat to supplement the regular fish diet. Of course, a few animals posed a problem, marauding packs of gray wolves, for instance, and the polar bear. A hungry wolf would attack a lone human, Greist states in his newsletter, and it was not unknown to have a ravenous pack of them invade a village. While less in evidence, polar bears could be encountered anywhere. Only the year before, one had blundered into Barrow at night, fallen asleep behind a storehouse, and was discovered there next morning. That set off a day of high excitement as a dozen Eskimos with spears and rifles pursued the startled and enraged animal through the village, and eventually out onto an ice floe, where it was cornered and killed.

Other excitements, especially concerning the health of the inhabitants, white and Eskimo, were not infrequent. One recent incident involved Joe Crosson and two little white girls seriously ill with dysentery—Greist wrote it up in his newsletter as "How Crosson Saved the Morris Children." The Morrises were a missionary couple stationed at Cape Halket, more than a hundred miles east along the coast from Barrow. Death was a real possibility for the little girls if they failed to reach a hospital promptly, the nearest one being at Barrow. A messenger was sent by dogsled to Sergeant Morgan, who flashed a wire to Joe Crosson in Fairbanks. As Greist explained in *The Northern Cross*, Crosson "at once left Fairbanks on the hazardous trip across the Endicott Mountains, through dense fogs, high winds, and other handicaps.

He was instructed to go directly to Cape Halket, pick up the children, and bring Mrs. Morris and the little ones to Barrow Hospital. And he did it, too, notwithstanding the overwhelming hazards." At the hospital, Dr. Greist and his wife did their part to save the little girls, who went home a few days later, recovered.

By now Greist had been living in Barrow for almost twenty years. He still didn't care for the primitive conditions, or the need to exist and do his missionary work on severely limited funds, all that the missionary board back home could afford (traveling by dogsled to bring the gospel to various other villages, he had his own troubles and adventures, including once being stranded for three days on an ice floe). But by now he'd become a staunch defender of the Far North as one of the world's most livable locations. "Florida is not the only health resort," he declared in a 1933 issue of his newsletter:

> . . . we can show as good results up here amid the ice and snow and Ozone. All we lack is a fifty-room hotel . . . a conservatory for fresh vegetables, or frequent plane service . . . and we would show the world what we can accomplish with our fresh reindeer, our invigorating atmosphere, the quiet, and the absence of much which makes for fast living in the states, such as movies, the bootlegger, the automobile, and late hours. . . . Here we live the simple life, know everyone by his first name, pay our debts, keep busy, and go to bed early . . .

Remote and isolated as it was, and aside from the ordinary excitements to be expected in so precarious a spot, Barrow also had its special moments, largely because of its location. It attracted famous visitors simply as a result of its being the northernmost settlement, and it also served as a staging area or jumping-off site for polar exploring expeditions. Most recently, in fact, only four years before the Rogers-Post journey, and at exactly the same time of year, mid-August, it had played host for three days to the world's most famous flyer, Charles Lindbergh, and his wife, Anne—at first in extremely anxious circumstances, but for Alaska not rare.

At the time the Lindberghs were making a Great Circle flight from New York to China, somewhat anticipating and perhaps even suggesting Wiley

Post's own Great Circle exploring flight from Los Angeles to Moscow by way of Alaska and the Bering Strait.

In August 1931 the two began by flying across the top of the Canadian mainland, stopping at Aklavik to refuel. They then flew on for Barrow as their last stop before crossing the Bering Strait into Asia. Soon after departing Aklavik they hit a patch of ugly weather, were seriously slowed, then became lost in thick fog. Unable to see or gauge the ground, uncertain about the weather ahead, they couldn't decide whether to turn back or chance going on to Barrow. That's where Sergeant Morgan and his wireless took a hand.

In the Lindbergh plane, Anne occupied the closed cockpit behind her husband. Working the shortwave telegraph was her responsibility. Her later picture of the episode, starting with the heavy fog that imperiled them, is graphic:

> . . . out to sea the white wall of fog stood impassable. Inland under floating islands of fog stretched the barren Arctic land. We were turning toward it as our only chance of reaching Point Barrow . . . Could we get through that night? If the weather ahead was not worse. I must get my message to the Barrow operator [it was Sgt. Morgan, though Anne of course didn't know who it was].
>
> "WXB—WXB—WXB," I called to him.
>
> "Dit-darr-dit!" A sharp, clean note came through my receiver. There he was! Right on the watch, though I had called him off schedule. Then there really was a man waiting for us. There really was a Point Barrow. We weren't jumping off into space. Somewhere ahead in that white wilderness a man was listening for us, guiding us in.
>
> Now my message: "Flying thru fog and rain going inland weather please."
>
> His notes came back clearly. I wrote rapidly not to miss a word: "Low fog bank rolling off ice now clear over fog expected soon pass ground visibility one mile." I poked the pad forward to my husband in the front cockpit. He glanced at it and nodded. That meant, "OK. That's what I wanted to know. We'll push on."

For hours they flew "through the unreal shifting world of soft mist . . . no sight of land, no sight of sea or sky." Only the instruments gave them any sense of the plane's position. Charles raised an arm and signaled for Anne to reel in the trailing antenna (a long wire with a weighted ball dropped from the plane's belly). If the plane was flying too low, or if they had to make a sudden landing, it could be snapped off. Two hours more of flying through fog followed, then Charles handed back a note: "Weather at Barrow?" Anne knew she couldn't let out more than a few feet of the antenna. That meant she couldn't send. She could only receive:

> . . . it all depended on the man at Barrow. If only he would go on sending in spite of our silence. We were powerless to let him know. "Weather . . . send us weather!" I pleaded mentally and put on my earphones.
>
> Silence. Wisps of fog scudded past us. No, there he was! "Darr-dit-darr, dit-dit-dit-dit," twice, three times, four times, then silence again, waiting for us to answer. I held my breath.
>
> There he was again! My pencil took down the letters, slowly spelling out the message: "Fog lifting fast visibility two miles don't think you have any trouble find lagoon." I poked my husband excitedly with the pad. That operator at Barrow—he did it—we'd get through all right now—Oh what a grand man!

The sense of responsibility that kept Sergeant Morgan sending when he wasn't sure anyone was listening, or that anyone needed it or cared, saved the Lindberghs in a very tight situation. If he had decided to close down for the night, since he was getting no reply, their China trip might easily have ended on an ice floe or in the freezing waters off Point Barrow, or with the plane lying as a heap of wreckage on the tundra.

When Lindbergh settled the plane easily on the placid Barrow lagoon it was just after ten p.m., August 8, 1931. There to greet them was the whole village, including most of the two hundred Eskimos. After introductions—shaking hands with Sergeant Morgan, Charles and Anne both thanked him profusely—they were taken to Dr. Greist's house. In the living room a table was being laid out for supper, white satin tablecloth and shining silverware. They'd be having reindeer meat, said Mrs. Greist proudly, and wild goose with sweet potatoes, peas, and beets.

Into the house crowded all nine members of the white community, "piling their parkas and sealskin boots at the door of the warm room." At the table, before the meal was served, Anne publicly thanked Sergeant Morgan for getting them down safely. That brought a loud round of applause, at which the sergeant smiled pleasantly and nodded. Anne found herself sitting next to the elderly Scotch whaleman, and, intrigued by his appearance and manner, tried to draw him out. He offered little but one-word replies smothered in good-natured growls, frowns, and harrumphs.

For two days the Lindberghs mingled with the villagers, Eskimos included, hearing their tales of life in the Arctic. Sergeant Morgan's infant son, they learned, was the first white child born in the area. Fittingly he'd been christened with the name of the village (Barrow Morgan lived for seventy years and died in Nome, Alaska, in 2001).

When the Lindberghs departed next day everyone was again on hand to see them off. As Anne bade Sergeant Morgan good-bye, she said she'd like to send him something. What would he like? There was nothing, he replied, thanking her. Then shyly he added that he wouldn't mind a pack of cigarettes. He'd run out a couple of weeks before.

Missing from that picture of the Lindberghs' visit is any mention of Barrow's own celebrity, the legendary Charles Brower. The reason is that he wasn't there at the time. He happened to be away, gone to Nome on Alaska's west coast to arrange some business and get supplies. Showing up a few days after the two guests left, he admitted he was sorry he'd missed the famous pair.

But Brower's own day was coming.

Almost precisely four years later he received the pleasant news that another pair of celebrities was headed for Barrow. This time it was to see and talk to *him*, Charlie Brower, King of the Arctic, and not just using it as a convenient stopping place or to enjoy the picturesque primitive surroundings. In his autobiography Brower recalls how on August 13, 1935, Sergeant Morgan brought him word of the impending honor:

Morgan hurried over to the station and handed me a message from Fairbanks. "Here you are, Charlie," he beamed. "Looks like we're due for visitors." I read the message and grinned back. Nothing could have pleased me better. Will Rogers and Wiley Post were planning to drop in on me, it said, and how was the weather up there? We flashed back word [about the weather] and began discussing their probable arrival . . .

The actual message, received from Fairbanks and written down by Sergeant Morgan in his radio shack, has not survived. But Brower's reaction to it allows for only one conclusion, that it was from Rogers himself, and it specified Brower by name as the renowned star's sole reason for traveling so far out of his way.

Who wouldn't grin!

5

AROUND THE TABLE in the Crossons' dining room in Fairbanks on the evening of August 12 sat four people talking and eating. There were Joe Crosson, and Lillian, his strikingly attractive wife, a relaxed Will Rogers and a fidgety Wiley Post. The Crossons' dog, a fox terrier, padded softly from chair to chair. "Name's Mickey," offered Crosson as Rogers stooped to pet him. The three Crosson children were in bed.

They were discussing where the two travelers had been since departing Juneau three days before, and Joe was surprised to hear that, after all the talk about it, they didn't stop at Skagway. Rogers explained that the total of twenty-two hours they spent in Dawson sort of made up for missing Skagway and its gold rush past. Dawson, too, had played a big role in the Rush of '98, and there were still some old-timers there who'd been a part of the excitement back then. Happily, Will had occupied most of an afternoon talking with them, that is, *listening* to them talk, an unfamiliar role for him. Best part of the trip so far, laughed Rogers, me keepin' shut an' hearin' men who can really talk an' who got somethin' to say!

Went up to Aklavik from Dawson, he went on, stayed overnight, met some Russians an' other people, saw a horse that ate fish an' walked on snowshoes, near froze to death in them howlin' winds, then flew off again an' here they were. "Almost went to Barrow 'steada coming down here, but Wiley says no an' he's the boss."

"Why not?" asked Crosson, looking at Post, who shrugged and mumbled, "Lousy weather."

Too bad they missed it, ventured Crosson. A whole different place. Something to remember. He'd been up there a few times himself. They'd lost their chance to see Charlie Brower, too, the King, in person. Brower was then at home, he'd heard. Be nice if Will *could* get up there and meet a man like Charlie, and give him a write-up. He'd been written about some already, but a story by Will would spread his name a lot farther. For knowing Alaska no white man could match him. Had Will read that book he'd given him, *Arctic Village*? On the way up to Barrow they'd fly right over that village, Wiseman, on the Koyukuk River. Crosson urged them to go down low and have a good look, maybe stop and meet the people. The way Marshall writes about it, Crosson added, he makes you *want* to go there!

But it was a tricky flight, ends Crosson, more so if the weather turns nasty, which it often did. I tell you what! Let me fly you up. I'll get one of the line's Fairchilds, a six-passenger job. Go in comfort. Stay overnight and—

"Thanks, Joe," interrupted Post. "I'd rather do my own flying. I mean if we go . . . that's up to Will . . . whether we go . . ."

Sure would like to go, put in Rogers. Sure would like to meet that old Brower. "I read some in the book. Does make you kinda curious. But we'd be sorta goin' backwards. How about it, Wiley?"

Up to you.

Sure?

Yeah. Up to you. . . .

You wouldn't mind?

Why should I mind . . . ?

Then we'll go!

Next morning Rogers had a message radioed to Brower in Barrow. He introduced himself, said maybe Brower had read in the papers about him and Wiley Post being in Alaska, said he'd heard so much about the King of the Arctic he couldn't hardly leave without meeting him, if that was OK. He and Wiley would be up that way soon as they had good weather, maybe the fourteenth or fifteenth, anyway pretty soon.

Brower's prompt answering wire, delivered to Rogers at the Pioneer Hotel, said that he and everyone else in Barrow would be happy to welcome the two famous wanderers. He hoped they'd be able to stay a while, and did Rogers ever eat reindeer meat? Nothing like a reindeer steak sizzling on the grill.

On the morning of August 14 the weather in Fairbanks was bright and sunny, but up in Barrow it was *very* bad. The usual morning report sent down from Barrow told of fog blanketing the entire area, which was often the case at that season on the Arctic shore, with zero visibility and a ceiling you could almost touch. Fog in Alaska wasn't the gentle gray mist it was in other places. Alaska fog in the Far North, people said, had *weight*. Walking through it you had to *push* it back.

Let's see what tomorrow's like, said Wiley, and Will agreed. Then the two made use of the extra time to do something memorable, fly in Crosson's plane over the snow-clad peak of lofty Mt. McKinley. (He'd never seen any sight more beautiful or spectacular, said Will, something he'd already said about the Inland Passage up to Juneau. Alaska was taking hold of him.) Then they flew down to Anchorage—where they were again surrounded by an admiring mob and shouting newsmen—and changed to a smaller plane for the trip to nearby Matanuska Valley, site of the federal government's relocation scheme for aiding indigent farm families in the Midwest.

During almost two hours at the settlement he talked to officials and to lots of farmers and their wives, then used the outing for one of his daily syndicated squibs. This one, however, carried a more serious message than most:

> Visited our new immigrants. Now this is no time to discuss whether it will succeed or whether it won't; whether it's farming country or whether it is not, and to enumerate the hundreds of

The last photo of Rogers, in Fairbanks the day before he died. Joe Crosson (hands in pockets), Wiley Post (top of head), Rogers (right).

Lillian Crosson often flew with her husband.

Joe, Lillian, and their children.

Lillian.

mistakes and confusions and rows and arguments, and manage-
ment of the whole thing at home and here.

As I see it there is but one problem now that they are here, and
that's to get 'em housed within six or eight weeks. Things have been
a terrible mess. They are getting 'em straightened out, but even now
not fast enough.

There is about 700 or 800 of 'em. About 200 went back; also
about that many workmen sent from the transient camps down
home (not CCC), and just lately they are using about 150 Alaskan
workers at regular wages. But it's just a few weeks to snow now, and
they have to be out of tents, both workmen and settlers.

You know, after all, there is a lot of difference in pioneering for
gold and pioneering for spinach.

Because it came from Rogers' hand, and received national exposure in
newspapers across the country, that mild complaint had its intended effect.
Within two weeks the Farm Bureau in Washington had prepared and distrib-
uted to papers everywhere a lengthy article on "Current Conditions in the
Matanuska Valley," promising that the settlers "will be comfortably housed
during the cold months." West Coast papers, especially, ran the piece at its
full length, along with photographs of the settlers at work (the *Oregonian*,
September 1, 1935, for instance).

Back in Fairbanks after writing the Matanuska squib, Rogers decided to
send a telegram to his family back east. Usually he wired news of his progress
to his wife, who by then was up in Maine, staying with their daughter, Mary
(still appearing at the Lakewood Theater in that play about a plane crash).
This time for some reason the telegram went to Mary, not to Mrs. Rogers. In
fact, for those few days in Fairbanks, Mary had been much on Will's mind.
In his pocket he carried a news story about her budding career, with a nice
photo, clipped recently from some paper. Several times he'd proudly shown
the clipping to the Crossons and others, a gesture that was particularly remembered by Lillian Crosson; "He was very sentimental," she recalled, "when
he looked at the picture of his daughter, a budding actress. I think I may have
reminded him of his daughter."

Quickly he wrote out the telegram and left it for Joe to send later:

> Mary Rogers, Skowhegan, Maine. Great trip. Wish you were along. How's your acting? You and Mama wire me all the news to Nome. Going to Point Barrow today. Furthest point of land on whole American continent. Lots of love. Don't worry. Dad.

Nome fronted the Bering Strait on Alaska's far west coast. It was the jumping-off spot for the planned Moscow flight, so mention of it can mean only one thing. The impatient Post had prevailed on his passenger to cut short their Alaska odyssey. After Barrow they'd head straight for Nome. Once there, apparently, Rogers would either part with Post and go home, or he'd stay and join the flight to Moscow. To now he still hadn't made up his mind.

The afternoon of August 15 found Rogers, Post, and Crosson together at the dock on the Chena River, the red seaplane floating nearby, all packed and ready. This time there was tension in the air, verging on anger, as Crosson tried to talk Post out of going. He should wait at least another day, insisted Crosson, until the weather at Barrow improved. For the tenth time that day, Post grumpily refused. It'll be all right, he shot back at his friend, I told you, it'll be OK! Rogers stood by in silence, deferring to Post as the expert.

That morning the weather report from Barrow had again noted a heavy fog shutting in the village and blotting out the landscape for miles around. Again it was ceiling zero, visibility zero. When Crosson passed the report to Post, he'd assumed that the trip would be called off for that day. But Post had impatiently brushed the report aside. By the time they got up there, he argued, say about seven that night, the fog would probably be blown off—this was the fourth day and it couldn't last much longer. Then if at any point he spotted trouble ahead he'd just set down on any one of the thousand lakes they'd be flying over, "open a can of chili and have a party." If he had to, he'd turn around and go back to Fairbanks.

No, Crosson warned, up here you don't figure the weather like that. You wait. You sit where you are and wait.

Yeah, yeah, came back the irritated Post. Listen, Joe, going around the world by myself I had to make a hundred quick decisions on weather.

He thought he knew what he was doing. He wasn't an idiot, wasn't crazy. They'd be OK. He'd make sure they kept out of fog. He wasn't going to risk a passenger like Will Rogers flying blind in fog.

Listen to me, Wiley, for once listen! You'll be flying over those Endicotts, and part of the Brooks Range. Like I told you last night you don't go up over those high peaks. You come down and use the passes, the ones I showed you on the map. What'll you do if the fog has drifted down from the north and you find yourself halfway through one of those chutes? What'll you do if the fog closes in behind you? Fog is sneaky like that.

Turning to Rogers, Post inquired, What about it, Will? This morning you said OK.

Rogers shook his head and shuffled his feet. Leave me out of it. I'm willin' if you think it's OK. What you said about sitting down if we have to on some lake sounds right. Makes sense. But you're the boss.

No, Will! resumed Crosson. If there's fog over Barrow you'll never find the place. Overshoot Barrow and you'll wind up in the middle of the Arctic Ocean or the North Pole! Wiley can't use the radio, either, can't send Morse while he's controlling a nose-heavy plane blind in a fog, even slowed down to eighty!

Oh, come on! snorted Post. Listen, Joe—

Do we *have* to go over this again? You admit that the plane is heavy up front because of that big engine. Then those new pontoons throw the balance even more out of whack. OK in fine weather, you can compensate. But it's not so easy lost in fog and fiddling with Morse at the same time. Wiley, you *know* I'm right!

"Yeah, Joe, yeah. But gimme some credit! I'm not an ama—"

Crosson shook his head resignedly. "OK. I'll fly you up myself, then. I'll get a Fairchild and fly you—"

"Thanks, Joe. I already told you no . . . thanks."

Another little problem still had to be dealt with. While flying to Fairbanks and landing on the Chena River, Post saw that there would be a problem when it came time to leave. One straight stretch of the river might accommodate a takeoff, but it wasn't near long enough for a plane carrying the full load of fuel that Wiley had aboard in those six tanks, 270 gallons. Room was needed to reach a safe liftoff speed, and then get airborne, and for this the Chena River wouldn't do.

The answer was simple: take off from the river with a half a load of fuel or less, then come down on some larger body of water where fuel was available, fill the tanks, and take off again. The larger body of water they chose was Harding Lake, about fifty miles southeast of Fairbanks.

With that, Crosson tried again. Would Wiley phone him from Harding Lake before taking off so he could hear Barrow's afternoon weather report? If it was still bad, or worse, wouldn't Wiley agree *then* to wait? In the four or five hours it'd take for him to get up there a heavy fog wouldn't be cleared off. A little, maybe, but not enough to make it safe.

What time in the afternoon is the report due? asked Post.

About one or a little after. By one thirty, anyway.

Post did a quick calculation and said he probably wouldn't get off from Harding Lake before two. OK, he said with a sigh, he'd phone.

At one o'clock in Fairbanks came the report from Barrow. No change. Visibility still zero. Ceiling zero. Also heavy rain and a snow squall moving in.

Any minute Wiley would be calling, thought Crosson sitting anxiously in his office at Pacific Alaska Airways. Now he'd *have* to give in and wait until next morning for another report.

At one fifteen there was no call. At one thirty no call. Crosson sat still, staring at the telephone on his desk. Five minutes went slowly by. Then he reached out and picked up the phone.

No, he was told, Post and Rogers weren't there. They had gone north, a nice, smooth takeoff. The crowd along the shore stood there watching until the plane had shrunk to a tiny red dot in the distance.

6

IN THE DRESSING ROOM she shared with two other girls in the cast of *Ceiling Zero*, Mary Rogers stood eyeing herself in the full-length mirror. Her trim figure was dressed prettily in the uniform of a Federal Airlines stewardess: slacks and a blouse, both dark blue. The first button on the neck of the blouse was open. For a moment she stared at it then reached up, opened the second button, and spread the collar a bit wider.

Curtain time at the Lakewood Theater in Skowhegan, Maine, was the usual one for summer stock, eight o'clock, and Mary was running a bit late. What held her up was a daylong rehearsal for the next week's bill, a whole new play—none of the dozen or so offerings listed for that summer of 1935 was scheduled to run for more than a week.

This was her second season at Lakewood, where each of the company's forty or so actors, a mixture of top pros and fledglings, was expected to take roles in some ten or a dozen plays. Originally it was her father's suggestion that she come here. When she first decided to try her luck on the stage, two years before, she was timid about it, confessing as much in a 1933 letter to her father. "You're right," she wrote, "this idea of going on the stage needs thought. It's hard to know what to do. Of course, ever since I've been a little girl I have thought vaguely of wanting to go on the stage. I keep thinking though that I haven't got enough *it*—I guess I lack self-confidence." (Movie star Clara Bow was known as the "It Girl," meaning a quality that blended charm, sex appeal, and a vivid personality.) Still, she said, she thought of going to New York and knocking on a few doors. Her sympathetic father had a better idea: "A stock company in one of those New England towns," he wrote her, "would be just the thing." In summer stock, he explained,

> they play different parts every week, and sometimes you might get right good, little parts, all depending on your ability. . . . [In New York] you might have just one or two little bits that you would have to do all summer. But it's stock where you get the real training . . . great memory and acting training . . . acting is experience, it's not learned in a day. . . .

A great admirer of her father, both as a man and a performer, emotionally and temperamentally close to him, Mary took his advice and applied to Lakewood for the 1934 season. The Rogers name, in fact, had as much to do with her acceptance as any acting talent she may have demonstrated—Lakewood openly favored the offspring of prominent actors. When her first few roles left her again in some doubt of herself, Rogers hurried to assure her in a letter that the reaction was only normal.

> How's my little actress sweetheart? Now don't you worry, stay with 'em and give 'em a little longer battle. . . . This will all do you good, and something good will come from it. This old being an actor or actress or being anything is not just what it's cracked up to be, you are going to get it on the chin time after time and you would get it in any other racket, and I think you are pretty game, and I am proud of you. That's as good and a lot better than running around here at all these night clubs and dances. . . .

In a later wire he reassures her with a single pointed sentence: "You got your old dad's good wishes sure you are nervous all good actors are nervous."

After a hectic 1934 season, maintaining many different roles, from bits to supports to leads, her hesitation about her abilities, about her possession of sufficient *it*, had completely melted away. She was an actress, and had proved it: comment in the local papers on her performances featured words like "clever" and "brilliant." She also scored a personal hit with the locals, the resort's permanent residents. "Mary is just one of us," declared one of them to the area's weekly, the *Somerset Reporter*. "She's just a lovable, unaffected girl." Really, they'd joke, Mary Rogers was just a very feminine copy of her father, and much prettier! She was also the possessor of that marvelous stage bonus, "a beautiful, controlled voice . . . she spoke as carefully as Bette Davis, only less testy, and almost as sultry as Lauren Bacall."

When the following year, 1935, she repeated the success of her first Lakewood summer, word arrived from New York offering her a good part in a new Broadway show that fall. She was on her way! she thought gleefully. It was partly her name that did the trick, she admitted, but who cared about that? She was an actress. She was on her way!

For *Ceiling Zero*, tonight would be the play's fourth performance of the week. Three more were to follow, one Friday night, and two on Saturday, including a matinee. The idea of appearing in a play about planes crashing had not appealed to Mary, not while her father was spending so much time in one flying over harsh terrain. But until she went up to Lakewood that April to prepare for the 1935 season, she hadn't known that *Ceiling Zero* was to be done, or that she'd be in it, and in any case her father hadn't said then that he'd be flying to Alaska, or flying anywhere.

When she was assigned to the cast of *Ceiling Zero*, and then heard about her father's Alaska plans, she'd thought of asking to be switched to something else. At last she brushed her fears aside as silly, amateurish. She was serious about her acting now. If she was going to be a professional, she scolded herself in concluding to stay in the *Ceiling Zero* cast, then she had to learn to conduct herself like one. A play was a play. It had nothing to do with your real life.

Anyway, Monday would see a change, with Mary in a new and completely different sort of role and glad of it, in a play called *The Little Inn*. The week after that she'd be starring as Sadie Thompson in Somerset Maugham's *Rain*. Then she'd have another four plays to learn and perform, and finally by the end of September she'd be done.

Good-bye Lakewood, hello Broadway!

Heading the cast of *Ceiling Zero* was a guest star from Broadway, a young man who'd just made a hit, his first, in New York in *The Petrified Forest*, named Humphrey Bogart. Other young hopefuls in the cast were, like Mary, the offspring of famous fathers or mothers. For instance, there was Keenan Wynn, making his stage debut. His father, the actor Ed Wynn, even then fondly known as "The Perfect Fool," was sitting nervously in the audience fidgeting as usual with his hands, his large, expressive features showing his anxiety to have his son do well.

In the audience was another well-known name, millionaire movie producer Howard Hughes, who had flown himself in that same day, "in a new plane he had just bought." A friend and visitor to the Rogers home, Hughes had already begun to show a more than friendly interest in young Mary. Also on hand was leading drama critic Bosley Crowther, of the *New York Times*, making his first visit to Lakewood.

LAKEWOOD
BRINGING BROADWAY TO MAINE

All Next Week Starting Monday Night, August 12
Matinee Saturday, August 17
LAKEWOOD PLAYERS PRESENT
The Sensational Aviation Drama

CEILING ZERO

By Frank Wead
with

Grant Mills — Humphrey Bogart

Mary Rogers	Converse Fenn
Joanna Roos	A. H. Van Buren
Kathleen Kidder	Owen Davis, Jr.

Two views of Mary Rogers, one as a teenager with her father, and the newspaper ad for the aviation drama in which she was starring the day her father crashed to his death.

Though in a countrified setting west of Bangor, Maine, on the shore of Lake Wesserunsett, the Lakewood Theater was not at all bare or spartan or bucolic. It was—and still is today—a legitimate professional setup with a well-designed stage and a spacious auditorium. "There is truly a flavor about the place of genuine camaraderie," wrote Crowther that night. "Lakewood is a summer resort or colony patronized by transient and permanent guests with the theater as its center. Yet the small group of actors, after all, is the tangible core of the place." When the 1935 season began, as usual on June 1, telegrams offering best wishes arrived from many prominent persons, Eleanor Roosevelt in the White House, for instance, George M. Cohan, and Will Rogers.

On the Lakewood stage, at precisely eight o'clock, as several latecomers hurried to their seats, the curtain parted. In her dressing room, Mary made a few last quick adjustments to her dark blue uniform, spread the open collar still wider, then checked her hair and makeup. She shrugged into a brown leather flying jacket, picked up a leather helmet, goggles, and gloves, then hurried out and took her place in the wings, mumbling her opening line.

The date is Thursday, August 15. In Alaska at that same moment, almost four thousand miles away, the little red plane carrying Mary's father is steadily droning northward, threading its way through the rugged and desolate peaks of the Endicott Mountains.

7

IN THE SMALL, cluttered Signal Corps radio shack at Barrow, Sergeant Morgan sits at his wireless set. In another chair sits Charlie Brower. It is the morning of August 15, and Morgan is sending the day's first weather report, indicating impossible conditions and heavy, widespread, blanketing fog. He finishes and turns to Brower.

Too bad, Charlie, Morgan comments lightly, looks like you won't get to play host to movie stars and celebrated pilots today. Not after that report to Fairbanks. Probably not for a few days. This stuff won't clear off in a hurry.

Brower nods. Hope the delay won't lead them to change their minds about coming here, he says. Be an awful disappointment to the ladies. Never saw them so happy about getting up a feast for visitors. Reindeer steak, Mollie says. Wonder if Rogers ever had reindeer. Do they sell reindeer meat in Hollywood?

At one o'clock that afternoon, Morgan again opened the wireless and sent the day's second weather report. No change, he wired, and spelled out the same impossible foggy conditions, with a ceiling that practically hugged the ground, along with a good chance of rain and snow. That was that, he thought. No visitors would be coming, not that day or for several more. Too bad if Rogers and Post decided they couldn't wait that long.

Aside from the flu epidemic earlier that year, nothing much out of the way or unduly exciting had happened in Barrow, not since the Lindberghs had dropped in four years ago. The summer of 1935 "was a busy but routine period at Barrow," later recalled Brower, a man who, even in his seventies, was pleased to have life take a daringly odd bounce now and then. "On the whole it was one of those uneventful periods which I have often noted about life in the far north; an interlude so suspiciously calm that after a while you find yourself bracing for the crash to come." On the fifteenth, after his meeting with Morgan at the radio shack, he and everyone else in the village "dropped back into the routine work of a nasty day." Mollie Greist opened the hospital doors to admit the waiting crowd, mostly Eskimo mothers with small children and infants. Frank Daugherty rang the school bell, then stood by the door as a mob of parka-clad boys and girls pushed in. Dr. Greist, helped by some Eskimo women, busied himself in the church, then went home to prepare his Sunday sermon. Eskimos on errands walked here and there in the fog-shrouded village, or worked on boats laid upside down on racks. The scene offshore to the north, out across the ice-clogged Arctic Ocean, was completely veiled by thick white fleece, softly billowing.

Later, the children let out of school played at front doors or in backyards or around the Eskimos' cozy sod huts with their whale-bone entrances. At evening, every smokestack and chimney was topped by a thin plume of grayish smoke as dinners were prepared. By ten o'clock an even deeper quiet settled down, the only light showing at the Daugherty house, a lamp glowing brightly in a single window. Beside it sat Frank Daugherty, reading.

Suddenly at the Daugherty front door a loud noise erupted, pounding and shouting. Dropping his book, Frank hurried to open it.

Outside stood an Eskimo, one that Daugherty recognized even in the darkness as a Barrow man. But he was panting heavily and his face, framed by a furry hood, glistened with sweat. It was Clair Okpeaha,* whose wife, Stella, helped teach the Barrow Sunday School.

"Airplane, she blow up!" shouted Okpeaha, waving his arms excitedly. "Airplane come down bad!"

"An airplane? It crashed?"

"Yes. Crash. Bad crash."

"Where?"

"Walakpa Lagoon. Ten mile." Okpeaha raised an arm and pointed to the southwest. "Two mans in."

"Two men? How do you know that?"

"Plane come down on water. Mans come out."

"They landed? They got out of the plane? But—"

"Then go back in plane, fly up, come down. Crash!" Okpeaha was still panting.

"Come in, come in. Here, sit down." Daugherty swung the door shut. "Quick," he urged, "tell me everything. We'll have to go out there. Are the men still alive?"

"In water plane turn over. I call long time, shout loud. Nobody hear."

"In water? Did it sink? Go down?"

"Water him not deep. Lagoon only little deep." He held his hands apart, indicating some three or four feet.

"You couldn't see anybody in the plane?"

"No see. Plane turn topside down. Bottom on top. No wheels. Little boats."

"No wheels? You mean floats, pontoons?"

"Yes. All broke."

---

* Oak-pe-a-ha

Daugherty reached for his parka. "You can tell me more later. Have to get out there. Clair, you go over to Charlie Brower and tell him. I'll get Stan Morgan. Tell Brower we'll have a boat ready. Faster by water, and we'll need to take some equipment. Then you come back here to show us where."

Okpeaha jumped up and ran for the door. "Clair!" called Daugherty. "When did it happen? How long you been running?"

"Maybe two hour. Not easy run rough place. Walakpa maybe ten mile."

Daugherty glanced at his watch. About two hours. Considering Okpeaha probably hadn't left there for ten, fifteen minutes, Daugherty estimated about seven thirty for the crash.

Outside, Okpeaha turned for the Brower station while Daugherty headed for the Morgan home. In five minutes Daugherty stood at the sergeant's front door talking to Beverly Morgan.

"He went out, Frank," she responded. "I'm not sure where."

"If he comes back tell him there's an airplane down at Walakpa Lagoon. Tell him I'm getting a boat ready and rounding up help. Tell him to meet me on the beach." He turned and hurried off, leaving Mrs. Morgan wondering at the door.

In his little workshop at the village's eastern end Brower was going through a pile of specimens, getting them ready for shipment "Outside," as Alaskans referred to anyplace not in their own sprawling state. Brower recalled:

> . . . there came a sharp knock followed immediately by the head-long entrance of a panting Eskimo named Clair Okpeaha. I knew Clair well, but had thought him away on a hunting trip. Whatever had brought him in on the run, it was plain from his face that something pretty serious had happened. Then as he caught his breath it came out that a plane had crashed in the lagoon. [Brower spoke Inuit, the Eskimo language, so the exchange with Okpeaha was more fluent.] . . . He'd run all the way and told Frank Daugherty, the schoolteacher, and Frank had sent him to me.
>
> Recovering his wind, Clair explained that he [with his family] was camping on a small stream at Walakpa when this plane flying low came overhead and passed back and forth several times . . . they

spotted Clair standing on the bank and a moment later brought the plane down on the lagoon. Then they waded ashore and asked him how far they were from Barrow. On learning that it was only twelve miles the two went back to their plane and took off.

They were up a couple of hundred feet [Clair expressed the height in his customary measurement, about fifty fathoms], when suddenly their engine sputtered and died. As Clair watched, the plane went into a nose dive, hitting the shallow lagoon with the speed of a rocket, and turning completely over, so that the engine and [part of the] fuselage were buried under three feet of water . . . the whole thing happened so quickly that he just stood there hardly able to believe his eyes. . . .

Okpeaha relayed Daugherty's message about a boat, then said, "Dogerty want me back," and turned to leave. Brower called after him that he'd use his own fast launch. "Tell Frank to go ahead. Tell him I'll send Dave [Brower's son] in the launch with some help and supplies, blankets, bandages, rope, tackle, you know."

As Okpeaha raced through the village he encountered a group of four or five Eskimos, his friends, stopped and blurted out the news of the crash. His halt lasting no more than a minute or two, he was about to run off again when Sergeant Morgan's tall form appeared at his side. "What's this about a crash, Clair?" he asked.

"Airplane. Walakpa Lagoon. I see. Dogerty go get boat. He want you too. You go beach. I go too."

Together, followed by the other Eskimos, Okpeaha and Morgan ran the short distance to the shore—at his house Morgan dashed in to grab his camera—where they found Daugherty and a dozen Eskimos with a large open whaleboat already in the water. Hastily Morgan and Okpeaha climbed in beside the schoolteacher, who revved the motor hanging on the vessel's transom. Slowly the heavily laden craft moved out, picking up speed as it went.

"Hampered by recent ice floes and strong adverse currents," Morgan later explained, and with a too-small motor on the big, overloaded, lumbering craft, "it took nearly three hours for us to reach our destination."

In their haste, strangely, they'd forgotten to take with them the only doctor in the village. Dr. Greist's annoyance at being overlooked in the emergency was still evident when, some weeks later, he recorded the night's events. He was "not even notified of the accident," be complained, and charged that Morgan and Daugherty "merely wished to get there, little knowing or considering what they could do on arrival." Apparently he'd been in bed asleep when Okpeaha got to the village, and had "accidentally learned of the wreck after all the boats had gone, and ran to the beach with first aid necessities but could not secure a boat, not even a skiff or canoe, man or lad, to help get him to the wreck." This neglect of Greist may not have been an oversight. He was an elderly man, liable to be overly moved and upset by a sudden, ugly incident. Perhaps there was a decision not to draw him from his bed into the Arctic night and ice-clogged waters, freezing temperatures, and possibly mangled bodies. The other two understood emergency medical procedures well enough.

But Greist's resentment was real, and the picture of him running along the shore, arms full of medical supplies as he hunted eagerly but in vain for a boat, is pathetic. He returned to the hospital, "and with the nurses, made ready for anything."

On the way to the wreck Morgan and Daugherty discovered who the two men in the plane might be, in fact, almost certainly were. Till then, speculation about the plane's occupants had centered on wealthy hunters out for polar bear—in fact, two such hunters had been in the Barrow area a month before. Other possibilities included newsmen chasing after an exclusive Rogers story. Questioning Okpeaha still more closely, Morgan asked him to describe the two men from the plane. Were they white men? Were they dressed like hunters? In suits like businessmen? Did they talk like Americans or did they sound foreign? It might have been a Russian plane drifted over from Siberia, he was thinking.

They didn't look like hunters, replied Okpeaha, not like any hunters he'd seen, not dressed like hunters. They were whites. One was bigger than the other. The smaller one got out of where the pilot sits, and he wore "a rag on his sore eye," something like a rag. A white rag.

Daugherty and Morgan looked sharply at each other. "Wiley Post!" cried Daugherty. "That eye patch! It's Rogers and Post!" Every newspaper photo of Post showed him with that conspicuous patch over his left eye. It was the best-known personal touch about him, how he'd lost an eye in an accident as a youngster and afterward always wore a patch, sometimes black, sometimes white.

"Which eye?" snapped Morgan. "Left or right? This one or that one?"

Okpeaha raised his open left hand and placed it over his left eye.

"Good God!" Morgan breathed softly, then quickly added, "But it *can't* be them! They had the two weather reports I sent today. With that kind of filthy weather staring them in the face they *wouldn't* try to come up here! Nobody in his right mind . . . it *can't* be them!"

Shortly before two in the morning the whaleboat rounded into the stream leading to the Walakpa Lagoon, which lay another curving quarter-mile ahead. The whaleboat's draft was not deep, so it slid along easily, only here and there lightly scraping bottom. As they proceeded, Daugherty looked through the half-light to his left and spotted at a distance a large white tent with a tall black smokestack sticking up through one corner of the roof. "That your tent, Clair?" he asked.

"My tent. Family there."

"Did any of them see the crash?"

"They see. All see."

"Was anyone else here who saw it?"

"No. Other hunters they go way."

"Before the crash?"

"Before."

"When the plane went up," asked Morgan, "was there anything wrong? Did the plane look OK? Anything bad? You've seen planes take off."

"Plane go up OK. Then motor go"—he used an Eskimo word, and accompanied it by a coughing sound, and a clapping of his hands. "Then plane turn." He raised a hand and demonstrated an arching, descending path. "Down. Crash."

"The motor stopped?" asked Daugherty.

"First strong motor, loud. Then"—he coughed again—"stop."

"Out of gas?" murmured Daugherty, looking at Morgan.

Photo from O'Brien, *Will Rogers*, 1935

Clair Okpeaha, Barrow Eskimo, who with his family witnessed the crash of Post's plane. Alone, he ran tirelessly to Barrow with the first news of the tragedy.

Walakpa Lagoon, west of
Barrow, where the Rogers-
Post plane crashed (at X).

A close-up of the crash
site (right) shows the
memorial monument
erected in 1938.

The wreck after the job of freeing Post's body.

Some of the Eskimos from Barrow who helped recover the two bodies from the wreck. The whaleboat ferried them between Barrow and Walakpa.

Eskimos in the vicinity of Walakpa Lagoon with the wreck in the distance, and the Arctic Ocean stretching north.

"Sounds like it," said the sergeant, shaking his head, "but how could that happen to a flyer like Post?"

Surrounded by what Daugherty called "a murky fog," and Morgan described as "dense fog and semidarkness," slowly they drifted into the shallow lagoon.

At its far end sat a tangle of wreckage. Sprawled upside down was a grotesque heap of shattered wood and metal, the crazily twisted pontoons lifted high atop the overturned fuselage, in the half-light seeming like some weird, enormous insect crushed to earth. For Sergeant Morgan the unreal scene presented "a most ghastly appearance and our minds chilled at the thought of what we might find."

Back at the stream's entrance appeared the Brower launch, holding Dave Brower with a half-dozen Eskimos. Loaded down with supplies, it had a large canoe in tow—the Eskimo variety called an *oomiak*, broad and light with only a few inches of draft. Dave had started from Barrow well after the other boat and had also encountered fields of pack ice, but had made good time. Chugging upstream, they drew alongside the stopped whaleboat.

Daugherty and Morgan had been about to bring their heavy craft up beside the fragile wreck. When they saw the oomiak behind the launch, they agreed that the lighter, more maneuverable canoe should be used, and that a couple of men—Morgan and young Brower—should enter the wreck first to see if anyone was alive. The oomiak was brought up, and Morgan and Dave stepped down into it. All understood that Sergeant Morgan was in charge.

The paddles raising barely a splash, the oomiak glided quietly over the water, came within twenty feet of the wreck, and halted. The lack of light and the twisted condition of the plane's parts made it hard to distinguish the craft's exact conformation and lie. The only obvious thing was that it lay upside down, the nose partly underwater and the tail, lifted by the rudder's thin top edge resting in the lagoon's shallow bottom, high in the air. The left wing was battered but still attached. The right wing was entirely missing and unseen, assumed to be lying flat underwater somewhere in the lagoon.

"Hello the plane!" called Morgan. "Anybody there? Can you hear me? Hello! Hello!"

Silence.

"Pass me that flashlight, Dave. Let's go aboard."

The oomiak slid over to the cabin's middle, where one window had been broken out. Reaching up, Morgan tried the little cabin door. It refused to budge.

"I'm too big to get in by that broken window, Dave," Morgan said. "Can you manage it? All the glass is gone, but be careful. Just take a quick look."

Aiming a flashlight through the window, Dave thrust his head and shoulders through, lifted a leg, and disappeared inside. Morgan moved forward in the oomiak and put his head through the window.

Climbing slowly over the scatter of debris, Dave inched back through the cabin toward the raised tail section. There was nobody, no sign of anyone. Turning, he crawled back down the sloping cabin toward the plane's nose. Still nobody. Then his flashlight shone over the inverted pilot's chair, causing him to draw back in fright.

Hanging upside down in the inverted chair was a man. Below his head, which was underwater, was the cockpit's shattered hatch cover. Pushed up against him was the plane's big engine, crushing him horribly.

Dave leaned down, put his hand gingerly on the back of the head, lifted it a few inches, and trained his flashlight on the face. Still covering the left eye was a white eye patch.

"It's him. It's Post. He's dead," said Dave.

"What about Rogers?" asked Morgan.

"Wait a minute." Dave moved about in the overturned cabin, searching around and under the debris. "Nobody else here, Sarge," he called finally.

Dave backed out of the broken window and let himself down into the oomiak. "Maybe Rogers survived and got out," he said hopefully. "Maybe he's somewhere off in the tundra looking for help."

"You sure you didn't miss him in there?"

"The cabin's not that big. Yeah, I'm sure."

Morgan threw a look around the lagoon. "If he did get out, he still must have been injured some. How would an injured man make it to shore in all this water? Could be he's lying out there somewhere at the bottom of this lagoon. Let's see what Frank thinks."

They rowed back to the whaleboat and announced the sad news that it was Rogers and Post, all right, with Post dead in the plane, but no sign of Rogers.

Daugherty suggested that Rogers might have been thrown out somehow by the impact of the crash, maybe as the plane flipped over. "There's a broken window in the cabin," replied Morgan, but he doubted the likelihood of Rogers being thrown out that way. "Dave, what about the four windows on the other side?"

"I think a couple are smashed."

"Possible to live through a crack-up like that, I suppose," observed Morgan quietly. "He'd have been sitting somewhere in the cabin. . . ."

"Should we try and dredge the water around the plane?" suggested Daugherty. "The water's not clear at all, so we'd have to probe. Do we have a hook?"

In the half-light the three men stand gazing around the placid gray surface of the shallow lagoon.

8

WITH MARY STILL IN THE WINGS at Lakewood awaiting her entrance, the first fifteen minutes of *Ceiling Zero* have passed. All the action has taken place in the office of Federal Airlines, in Newark, New Jersey (the three-act play has only a single set, the office). At about center stage is the desk of the line's supervisor, Jake Lee. At other desks sit two operations men, Buzz and Doc.

In the play Bogart is Dizzy Davis, a crack aviator but a charming scamp who breaks all the rules and has a roving eye for the ladies. The play centers around Davis, whose actions cause two fatal crashes, including his own. The first crash occurs one stormy night as Bogart/Davis dallies with the girlfriend of another pilot—Mary Rogers is the girlfriend—and his best friend has to fly the plane in his place. Contrite after the friend crashes and dies, Davis tries to make amends by piloting an especially hazardous flight, taking another pilot's place after knocking him cold. His dangerous mission is to test a new wing deicing device. If it fails, a crack-up is possible, even likely. The device does fail, and Davis crashes and dies.

The two crashes—the play's dramatic high points—are made vivid to the audience by reports from the planes in flight coming in through an office loudspeaker, and by the reactions of the characters on stage.

Mary is Tommy Thomas, a stewardess at Federal, who has also been taking flying lessons in an open-cockpit plane from a few of Federal's pilots—the script describes her as "a thoroughly grand kid and the type that almost any guy would like to get acquainted with." In her hands now she holds helmet, goggles, gloves, and a white scarf. Jake is talking. Mary hears her cue and rushes out.

> TOMMY. Hey, you mug! I've flown! For the first time! I've soloed, Jake! I've soloed!
>
> JAKE, *with mock severity.* Mug? Is that any way for an air hostess to address her boss?
>
> TOMMY *grabs Jake by the shoulders and snuggles up to him affectionately.* Aw, Jake, don't be so dignified. *(Puts gear on desk.)* I've waited for this for weeks, for months—forever! *(Removes coat.)* Now I'm a fledgling! Aren't you proud of me? Aren't I sumpin?
>
> JAKE. I'm sure you'll be a credit to the industry.

After another ten minutes, Bogart as Dizzy Davis enters and from there on the plot focuses on him and his attentions to Mary as Tommy. Full of breezy comment and relentlessly snappy dialogue, the first scene uses the office loudspeaker several times, with the operations men talking to the pilots in flight. At the close of Scene Two comes the first crash, in a sequence that builds for some eight minutes to a shattering climax. The plane is lost in fog, and Jake is in the office trying to talk it down to a safe landing. The suspense is built by the interplay between frantic office comments and the pilot's voice crackling urgently over the loudspeaker, with the deep-throated drone of the engine heard in the background:

JAKE, *(into transmitter.)* You're coming into the field, Tex! Toward Number One hangar! Keep her straight and settle in low. *(The DRONE increases. Baldy holds up two fingers and shows them to Doc.)*

JAKE, *(into transmitter.)* You haven't reached the edge of the field yet! Tex, your altimeter should read two hundred feet. Keep her straight and steady! *(The DRONE increases. They all listen.)*

LOUDSPEAKER. *(Tex's voice is faint and garbled.)* Here I come. Feeling for the ground. Why don't you answer? It's a wonder you wouldn't help a fella. *(The DRONE increases.)*

JAKE, *(into transmitter.)* Pull her up a little. Pull her up! Tex—you sound low. You're still outside the field! Watch it! Pull her up, Tex!

BALDY. He sure sounds low.

Doc, *(sharply.)* He's right on top of the hangar!

JAKE, *(frantically into transmitter.)* Pull up, Tex, pull up! You're too low!

TOMMY, *(shouting.)* Tex! Look out! . . .

From the loudspeaker, echoing harshly through the theater, comes the terrible sound of a plane hitting the ground, described in the script as "a terrific, metallic, tearing CRASH as the plane rips into the hangar, the boom-boom of exploding gas banks, and a burst of flame flickering distantly through the fog in the windows at right. All lights in the office go out except small emergency lights. . . . Buzz reaches up and turns on the crash siren, which shrieks in growing crescendo."

Whatever the scene may look like on paper, when it played at the Music Box on Broadway the previous spring it won raves. "One of the most exciting second act climaxes of melodrama's recent history," the *New York Sun* called it. The *New York Journal* went further: "at the end of the second act the play holds all the screeching terror and mute impalpable doom that hang with a dead weight and mortal danger in the dead mist of a fog bank. It is Guignol

The two plane crash scenes from *Ceiling Zero* as originally played on Broadway. The audience heard the doomed pilots' voices, and the sound of the crashes over loudspeakers on the set. Mary's character was on stage for both crashes.

stuff, if you please, but effective, racking, terrifying, with all the subtlety of a torture chamber."

Counting rehearsals, Mary had now listened to that awful, racking sound at least nine or ten times.

The play began with an eight o'clock curtain, so this crash, the first of two in the play, occurred at nearly ten-thirty, Maine time. Up in Alaska, at the Walakpa Lagoon just west of Barrow, the time was earlier, about six-thirty. The little red plane was nearly five hours out of Fairbanks, and by now should have sighted Barrow in the distance. But like the doomed plane in *Ceiling Zero* it was lost in thick fog.

On the Lakewood stage, some thirty minutes later, comes the second crash, the one that kills Bogart/Davis. Briefer, lasting some five minutes, it is more subtly done, increasing its impact. The loudspeaker's role is the same, but the sound of the crash itself is not heard. Again the exchange is between Jake and the loudspeaker. The time at Lakewood is about eleven-fifteen. At foggy Walakpa Lagoon it is four hours earlier, about seven-fifteen. Post and Rogers have just finished talking with Okpeaha and have climbed up into the plane. Post, in the cockpit, throws back a farewell wave, shuts the canopy, taxies away to a distance, turns, revs the engine, and takes off, rising sharply into the air.

On stage at Lakewood the voice of Bogart/Davis comes chillingly through the loudspeaker: "The old ship won't stay with it much longer, Jake. Ice looks a foot thick on the leading edges. I'm down to fifteen hundred feet."

> JAKE, *(into transmitter.)* Can't you nurse her down! Slide in on a wing so it'll be an easy crack-up? Do something, Dizzy! Anything!
>
> LOUDSPEAKER *(Dizzy's voice.)* She's getting wishy. Won't answer the controls. Just starting to spin. Give my love to Fred Adams. I hope the boys like the Brownings. G'bye, gang. So long Jake. Maybe you won't believe— *(STATIC)*
>
> JAKE, *(into transmitter.)* Dizzy! Newark to Davis in Seven! Newark to Davis in Seven! Answer Seven! Answer! Seven! *(There is no answer. They realize Dizzy is dead. Jake turns away, hands the*

*microphone to Buzz, turns to the panel board and leans against it,
tense and broken.)*

At Walakpa, as the rising plane reaches a hundred feet, the engine suddenly begins to miss, cutting rapidly in and out—stopping, loudly restarting,
stopping, starting—then the roar halts entirely and there is only silence as the
plane noses over and plunges toward the ground.

On stage at Lakewood, after some lines of wrap-up dialogue are heard, the
curtain closes to a burst of hearty applause. Lazily, still in their minds hearing
the ominous crackling of the loudspeaker static, people get up and begin to
drift toward the exits. In minutes the theater is empty and quiet. In her dressing room, Mary changes clothes, says good night to the others, and leaves.

Alone, enjoying the soft warmth of the moonlit night as she comes down
from the excitement of her performance, she walks the few minutes from the
theater to the cottage by the lake. She opens the front door and is greeted
by her mother and her aunt Theda. Usually the two see Mary's every performance of every play. But they'd seen *Ceiling Zero* its first night, couldn't keep
from thinking of Will, and never went back.

There's a wire for her from Dad, says Mrs. Rogers. Nothing important. Just
a little greeting and a report on his plans. Mary accepts the Western Union
telegram and reads what her father had written that morning before leaving
Fairbanks for Barrow. "Great trip. Wish you were along. How's your acting?
You and Mama wire me all the news to Nome. Going to Point Barrow today . . . lots of love. Don't worry."

"That part about Nome," says Betty, appearing more than a little disap-
pointed. "Looks like Dad has made up his mind about going on with Wiley.
I was hoping he'd have had enough of vagabonding by now and would come
here. Now I'll have to fly home and pack and ask him where he wants me to
meet him. Hope it's not Moscow! London I wouldn't mind, or Paris. He'll
probably wire us again from Nome."

The next morning all three women are up early as usual. Mary goes off
for rehearsal of her next week's role. Her mother and aunt stroll over to visit
the Arthur Byrons in their big place on the lake. Ten minutes later they are
all sitting on the Byrons' front porch, with Betty explaining how she'll be off

for Europe in a few days to meet Will, when a car drives up and halts at the porch steps.

The car door opens and out step two sober-faced men—Carlton Miles, the Lakewood publicity director, and Humphrey Bogart. From her seat on the porch Betty calls out a cheerful good morning, adding that Mary isn't there.

My, they're looking awfully grim this morning, she thinks as the two come up the steps. Bogie especially with that lean, hard, expressive face of his. He doesn't really fit the part of the playboyish Dizzy Davis, she decides. Of course, in summer stock you don't worry about that. You try different things.

9

"Nothing," mumbled Sergeant Morgan to Frank Daugherty as he stepped up from the oomiak into the whaleboat, followed by Dave. "Not a thing."

He dropped the long pole across the seats. "Can't probe every foot of this lagoon," he added, eyes sweeping along the darkened shore. He shook his head in frustration. "Can't see anything from out here. Let's go look along in there. He might have made it that far. Dave, you and Clair go off to the left and work around that way. We'll go to the right. Anybody finds anything, call out."

As the four began moving across the open water a shout came out of the gloom, an Eskimo hailing a word that all recognize. From the opposite shore an oomiak heads toward them. "My son," said Okpeaha, peering through the murk.

As the oomiak slid closer, the young Eskimo in it began yelling a stream of excited Inuit words, finishing as he drifted alongside the whaleboat. Okpeaha pointed to shore and said quietly, "Other man there. He dead."

Morgan and Daugherty hurried into their oomiak, while Dave and Okpeaha climbed down into the son's. Quickly they rowed, led by young Okpeaha, and as they neared land they could see what appeared to be a covered body lying flat, with its feet toward the water. As the oomiaks beached, the occupants hastened ashore.

It was certainly a body. Enclosed in a sleeping bag, it was also loosely wrapped in canvas. Kneeling down, Morgan pulled away a corner of the canvas, then took hold of the sleeping bag's zipper and yanked it down, revealing a face badly bloodied. On cheeks, nose, lips, and forehead were deep lacerations. Part of the scalp was torn loose and the top of the skull was slightly crushed.

Daugherty leaned over to look. "Is it him?"

"It's him," said Morgan through clamped lips.

Turning to Okpeaha, Daugherty asked, "Does your son know how the body got here, on shore like this?"

Okpeaha spoke a few Inuit words to his son, which prompted a lengthy reply. When the boy finished, Okpeaha said, "Hunters come long take dead man from plane. After me go. Eskimo hunters. They look plane. Take dead man out. Other dead man can't get."

"Your son saw them?" asked Daugherty.

"In tent. No see. They bring white man things from plane."

"Things?"

"Big bag like box, books, little machine, papers, pole for fish. Bag to sleep. Broke guns."

They could go into those details later, interrupted Morgan. Now they had to finish their task of getting the bodies back to Barrow, arrange to get them back home. They had to notify the two families . . . and the world had to know.

Daugherty wasn't convinced about the hunters. The boy might have been wrong about where they found the body, he thought. Why would Eskimo hunters go into a wreck, take out a dead body, and lay it on the shore? More likely they found it on the shore and covered it up, then retrieved belongings from the plane. It seemed obvious to him that when the falling craft "struck the rough terrain near the river bank and bounded over, Rogers' body was catapulted away from the plane." Or as he phrased it elsewhere, "Rogers' body was hurled from the crashed ship as it somersaulted among the hummocks near the river." How it exited the plane was a different problem.

Okpeaha, hearing Daugherty say as much to Morgan, waved his hands vigorously. "No, no," he said. "Hunters take from plane. They mans I see when I run Barrow. I tell them plane crash."

Daugherty's look still said maybe.

Extracting Post's body from the collapsed upside-down cockpit required a special effort, long and terrible. The uplifted pontoons blocked access to the plane's underside (now facing up), and had to be moved out of the way. For this, long ropes were attached to the pontoons and pulled by a gang of Eskimos on shore. Then an opening had to be made in the bared metal. Engine and pilot's seat were each moved slightly, again by a strenuous rope pulling by the Eskimos, giving just enough room to free the mutilated body. Dave Brower and a husky young Eskimo named Rex Ahvakana performed the gruesome task. "Dave and I had to almost dive down to get the body out," Ahvakana recalled years later. "We didn't want to tear up his body too much. It was cold. We were down in the water about arm's length and somebody was holding our boots and we were upside down. We broke one of the floats down to get him out. We finally freed him around early morning."

Swathed in blankets, now blood-soaked, the body was passed down into the whaleboat and sealed in a sleeping bag. Ashore, it was laid on the frozen tundra beside the body of Rogers, as Morgan and Daugherty discussed which boat the two should be taken back in.

Before leaving, Morgan took out his camera and made a series of shots from different angles of both the wreck and the two bodies on the shore. His habit was to make a photographic record of anything and everything that struck him as out of the way. Daugherty and Dave also took photos.

The rescue party's return to Barrow along the curving shoreline was nearly free of the obstacle of pack ice, and the boats now ran with the current, so the trip back was made in well under two hours. When they arrived at the Barrow beach it was just after four a.m. In the bottom of the towed oomiak were the two wrapped and covered bodies, lying end to end, with a young Eskimo sitting at the bow and another at the stern.

As the boats floated up to the beach, the soft sound of their throttled-down motors rode the still night air and was heard by the anxiously waiting Brower and Dr. Greist. Then over the low thrum of the engines they heard other sounds, the guttural chanting of Eskimo voices, all those in the boats. The dead men had been nothing to the Eskimos—they had never even heard the names before—but they could see how their white friends were affected, so they were joining in their sorrow.

Together, wrote Greist, he and Brower stood

> . . . upon the high veranda of the hospital awaiting word of the return of the relief party. At that moment we heard . . . a weird and most beautiful chant, a hymn of the ancient Eskimo, sung only for and in the presence of the honored dead. . . .
>
> Arriving at the beach the boat containing the bodies was lifted out of the water by some twenty young Eskimos, carried up over a sandspit, and placed in the waters of the lagoon, then paddled to the landing at the very foot of the stairway to the hospital. The bodies on stretchers were carried by silent young men to the operating room. . . .

The unexpected news that the dead men were Rogers and Post came with terrific impact to the waiting whites, especially the four wives. Brower, who as U.S. Commissioner had official charge of the bodies, remembered the moment. The fact that the motors of the returning boats were not opened wide but were running at normal speed seemed ominous:

> . . . a glance at the two heavily wrapped forms lying in the bottom of the oomiak offered mute proof that the worst had happened. And yet I was hardly prepared for the shock that Dave's first words brought.
>
> "Dad," he said, "it's Will Rogers and Wiley Post!"
>
> It couldn't be! The weather reports we'd sent—"How do you know it's them?" I asked, forgetting that the two would be quite as familiar to Dave as to thousands of other countrymen all over the world.

Morgan explained how Okpeaha's mention of the eye patch on the way down had betrayed the truth, and that sight of the two had confirmed the sad news.

Eskimos watching over the bodies of Rogers and Post, lying on the shore of Walakpa Lagoon.

The two bodies with the upside-down plane wreck in the background.

Directed by David Brower, Eskimos from Barrow dismantle the wreck.

Part of the wrecked plane taken ashore. The engine was also recovered, and after cleaning and repair was put back in service on another plane.

The little hospital had been in a flurry of preparation, readying itself to receive two injured accident victims, a necessary assumption. With the arrival of cadavers instead, the tension in the hospital eased off. The work now was repairing corpses, getting them cleaned and in proper shape for their return home. For that gruesome task there was no need to hurry.

At home the wives, Eskimo and white, cooked up big batches of stew and baked and sliced bread interminably—the numerous rescue party would be tired, hungry, and cold. Large at the outset, it had steadily grown in size as boat after boat put out for Walakpa Lagoon. If more help was needed, no Eskimo man cared to be left out, and it was later found that almost all the village's Eskimo men went to the accident site that night.

On hand at the hospital was Charlie Brower. His acquaintance with every sort of Arctic situation was extensive, including physical injuries and their care. Still more helpful would be his steadying influence on the others, in particular Dr. Greist who, said Brower, "was an old man and this certainly upset him . . . and for once [he was] so nervous that he could hardly work." But work the faithful Greist did, staying in the operating room continuously for five hours until the task was finished. Mollie Greist was there too, assisting, especially to thread the needles for what seemed the endless sewing of torn flesh.

Rogers' body was cared for first. Placed on the operating table, it was stripped of its clothing—cut away, mostly, all of it now ripped, dirty, full of sand, and bloodied (a double-breasted business suit of light gray, white shirt, and a tie). The high rubber boots were unlaced, but getting them off was difficult since both legs from the knee down had been broken. The torso was bruised and battered but intact. His left hip had a deep laceration, and his left arm was broken. The worst injuries were to his head: the face and ears were cut and otherwise damaged, and the top of the skull was partially crushed and the scalp torn.

Mollie Greist went through Rogers' pockets, in both jacket and trousers. He had more than seven hundred dollars in cash and more than two thousand dollars in traveler's checks. There was also a pocketknife, a small reading glass, a stubby pencil, a metal sales token, a small puzzle made of paper and wood, and two watches. One of the watches, the cheap, two-dollar pocket type, was attached by a piece of string to a buttonhole. It was still running, as was the other, more expensive watch.

With the work finished, Rogers' body was removed from the operating table and replaced by Post's, now with the white eye patch removed, showing the left eye to be an empty socket. Post's wounds, inflicted on chest and abdomen by the crushing weight of the engine, were more massive than Rogers', and had obviously been instantly fatal.

By the dim glow of a random array of low-wattage lamps, run on the hospital's own generator, the Greists, Brower, and Daugherty, aided by an efficient group of Eskimo women, patched up the many tears and breaks in both bodies as well as they could, removing or straightening fragments of bone. Special attention was given to lessening the appearance of trauma on both of the well-known faces. Finally both bodies were dressed in the only proper garments available, long woolen white nightgowns.

It was nine o'clock in the morning of Friday, August 16, before both bodies lay on tables, swathed further in fresh white sheets and blankets, with an outer covering of canvas. By noon they had been carried to a storage shed behind the Brower house, where the natural refrigeration would preserve them until they could be flown back to Fairbanks.

Those five hours in the small, crowded yet silent operating room was an emotional experience for all concerned, but especially for the elderly Rev. Greist as doctor in charge. Later he would write in his newsletter that "not in many years, probably never, has this village been so shocked, so stunned beyond expression" as it was by the Rogers/Post tragedy. All in the isolated little community

> . . . had fondly hoped to entertain Messrs Rogers and Post on their arrival at this far outpost of civilization, and that to the utmost extent of our modest ability. We had planned great things in their honor . . . we had hoped to place before these noted travelers such a feast by way of venison and wildfowl as would prove worthy. But, alas! The saddest [words] of all, it might have been.
>
> We but sorrow with the bereaved families, and would have them know that we did our best for their loved ones, that we worked over

their torn bodies as with sacred things, and forgot not. Words are so inadequate, fall so far short of being even symbols of ideas, and they fail us. But our hearts are with the suffering.

That evening a white trader who had just arrived in the village from down the coast, a man named Gus Masik, went to Brower's place to do some business. In casual talk with Eskimos on the way he learned of the plane wreck, and when talking with Brower he offered information that he thought might help piece together the story of the accident. The day before, he explained, he'd been in a boat crossing Smith's Bay—a miles-wide indentation in the coast well to the east of Barrow—in heavy fog that covered the bay almost down to its surface. When he was about halfway across he heard the roar of an airplane motor high overhead, obscured by the thick mist. He saw nothing and the sound lasted only a couple of minutes—seeming to go in wide circles before it began fading away to the west.

At the time Masik said he wondered who would be foolish enough to fly in such weather, and it looked like the poor beggar, whoever he was, paid a high price for his mistake. When Brower told him who was in the plane he could only shake his head at the thought of two famous men needlessly dying like that.

Sergeant Morgan had not aided in the preparation of the bodies. Instead, for all those hours through the night he had sat tirelessly in his radio shack telegraphing the terrible news, first to his chief at the Signal Corps station in Seattle, then answering the flood of inquiries that poured in from individual newspapers, news services such as the Associated Press and the United Press, radio stations, photo agencies, and individuals. For most of the next two days Morgan's hand would seldom be off the telegraph key.

His initial message, sent to Colonel George Kumpe of the Signal Corps in Seattle for transmittal to Mrs. Rogers and Mrs. Post, had gone out soon after the return to Barrow from Walakpa. It was short and to the point: "Post and Rogers crashed fifteen miles south here eight p.m. last night. Both killed. Have recovered bodies and placed care of Dr. Greist." As the night wore on he sent lengthier, more detailed reports, gradually filling in the story of that mournful night.

Colonel Kumpe's wire to each of the two wives, quoting Morgan's first brief message, went out from Seattle just before six that morning. The Rogers wire, flashed to the family's Santa Monica home, was rerouted to the Lakewood cottage in Skowhegan. Before it arrived, the awful news had reached the shocked ears of Lakewood's publicity man, Carlton Miles. Arriving at the theater that morning, he caught it as a bulletin on his office radio.

Rushing out to his car, he stopped in the lobby to snatch from a table the regular early edition of the *Bangor Daily News*. The page-one streamer headline read *Will Rogers and Wiley Post Meet Tragic End*.

"Carl!" blurted Humphrey Bogart, hurrying into the lobby, "Mary's father is dead! A plane crash! I just took a call from Alaska, Rex Beach in Juneau. He wanted to speak to Betty but I . . . his plane crashed last night! Rogers is dead!"

Silently, Miles handed him the paper.

10

FOR A MOMENT BETTY stared blankly at Bogart's familiar but now haggard features. Then she switched her gaze to Carlton Miles' strained countenance. Suddenly she moved, her body jerking violently as if shaken by a convulsion.

"She doubled over," said Bogart, recalling Betty's reaction when he told her that Will was dead, "as if I'd hit her."

When the two men first arrived at the Byrons' cottage on the lake, Miles took Theda aside, escorting her down the steps and off to the side of the house for privacy. He wanted her advice on how to approach Betty with the devastating news, but just telling Theda proved difficult. Still, as he said afterward, Betty suspected something "at once," by the manner of the two men. When Miles took Theda aside, Betty's alarm turned to panic, at the thought that something had happened to her son Jim, then driving with a cousin cross-country from California to join her in Skowhegan. Betty herself later described the moment:

> I ran after them. Something had happened to Jimmy. The boys had been in an accident—I was sure of it. My sister said, "No, Betty, it's Will. Will has had an accident."
>
> For a moment I felt only relief. Nothing could happen to Will. A forced landing or an exaggerated report of some trouble with the plane. Jimmy was safe, and nothing could happen to Will. . . .

"Come inside, Betty," said Theda, taking her sister's arm. "I'll tell you."

All six people in the little group moved into the Byrons' living room. It wasn't just a little accident, said Bogart hesitantly to Betty . . . there'd been a crash . . . a bad crash . . . Will had not survived it . . . Will was . . . dead. . . .

The words shook Betty off her feet. Miles and Bogart each took an arm and led her to a sofa where she sat in the tight embrace of her sister, softly moaning. Outside at the door of the cottage people came crowding up, among them actor Keenan Wynn and playwright Owen Davis and his wife. (Mary had taken parts in several of Davis' plays at Lakewood.)

"Where's Mary?" asked Davis, turning to Arthur Byron.

"Rehearsing next week's play. At the theater."

With Miles at the wheel, and Aunt Theda, Davis, and his wife in the car, the drive to the theater took hardly a minute. In the auditorium they found Mary on the bare stage with several others, a scatter of chairs and tables simulating the set. "Not until she had finished the scene then in progress," explained the *Somerset Reporter* the next day, "did they quietly draw her aside and suggest her return to the Rogers cottage. There the news was broken to her by her Aunt Theda." Bogart, watching warily, saw with concern that the girl appeared "stunned." Wide-eyed and frozen, she sat silently staring.

No other description of Mary's reaction is on record anywhere. Only available are a few stray hints in news stories, all pointing to a devastating impact on the young girl. For the return to California, she would only go by train, she said, though her mother and her aunt felt that the three-day journey would be a slow, nervous ordeal. Offers made by several people to fly them home, noted the *Reporter*, had been refused: "Mrs. Rogers was on the point of accepting,

Mary Rogers Plays Leading Role in Air Crash Drama as Her Father Falls to His Death in Alaska Flight

Ceiling Zero, a Former Broadway Success Produced at Lakewood, Me., Features a Plane Accident Off Stage.

By the United Press.

LAKEWOOD, Me., Aug. 16.—Will Rogers' wife and his pretty actress-daughter, Mary, bore up bravely here today as they listened to the news of his death in an Alaskan airplane crash.

Ironically, Mary has been playing the feminine lead in the Lakewood Players' presentation of the Broadway success, "Ceiling Zero," a thrilling aviation drama. A feature of the play is an off-stage plane crash in which a pilot is killed.

Mrs. Rogers today telephoned friends in New York that she would leave as soon as possible for the Rogers home in California, says the Associated Press. She telephoned that she would leave for the coast not later than tomorrow. Mrs. Rogers and her daughter, Mary, will be accompanied West by Dorothy Stone, daughter of Fred Stone.]

Neither the cowboy humorist's young daughter nor his wife, the former Betty Blake of Rogers, Ark., who arrived here Tuesday, commented when the news was broken to them by a theater attache. The report had been withheld until confirmed by the United Press.

With them at the time, at the home of friends, was Miss Theda Blake, of Beverly Hills, Cal., a sister of Mrs. Rogers.

Mary's brother, James, was due here tomorrow.

The family's plans as a result of the tragedy were not immediately announced.

"Ceiling Zero" is only one of several plays in which Miss Rogers has appeared here this summer.

By the Associated Press.

LOS ANGELES, Aug. 16.—Will, Jr., 23-year-old son of Will Rogers, about to sail on a short cruise aboard an oil tanker, was sent rushing home to Beverly Hills today by the report, "some kind of an accident has happened to your father."

Officials of the Standard Oil Co., aboard whose ship W. M. Story, young Rogers had spent the night at dock in the harbor, said they had not informed Will of his father's death.

Will had planned to sail on the tanker to Estero Bay, approximately 100 miles north of here.

By the United Press.

CHELSEA, Okla., Aug. 16.—Mrs. Tom McSpadden, 70-year-old sister of Will Rogers, collapsed today when informed that her brother had been killed. Her condition was described as serious.

The coincidence of Mary's appearing in a play about plane crashes was well reported, but in subdued terms. No one at first realized the true, tragic depth of her shock.

STAGE PLAYS.

This photo of Mary appeared in the *New York Times* during her gallant effort in 1935–1936 to resume her acting career.

but Mary, shocked and unnerved by the air tragedy, insisted the trip be made by train." The *Reporter* also noted that Mary had appeared in "the air drama *Ceiling Zero . . .* this play vividly brought to mind the nerve wracking experiences of those who watch helplessly as their loved ones meet death in a plane crash." In New York, her brother Jim was seen "gently aiding the girl into a waiting cab. Pale, she showed the strain of her ordeal."

Before they left Lakewood for home late on Friday, noted the *Reporter*, the three grief-stricken women

> remained in seclusion during the afternoon and evening. Meantime news agencies the world over thundered at the gates of Lakewood with morbid requests for the story of the Rogers' reactions to this great tragedy. Over 2000 telegrams and hundreds of phone calls arrived. One from a London newspaper.
>
> But the Rogers were carefully shielded against prying newsmen and photographers, and only the terse statement that they had taken their loss "bravely" was given out.

One aggressive reporter for the *Bangor Daily News* tried to breach their seclusion and failed. Locked away in their cottage, he wrote, "They would see nobody. They had no plans. The tragedy was too sudden. Alone, they mourned the death of a husband, father, and brother-in-law, and waited for son James, who is enroute here."

More concerned with the reaction of the youthful, vulnerable Mary, the *Somerset Reporter* concluded its initial coverage of the tragedy by offering her encouragement:

> What will be Mary's plans for the future no one here knows. It is expected that following the funeral of her father she will for a time go into seclusion with her mother at the palatial Rogers estate in California. It was generally agreed that Miss Rogers, who but two summers ago was a novice of the stage, had made rapid strides and was headed for starring parts on Broadway this fall.
>
> Whether she will be able to go on with her work so soon after this shocking incident is not known. As Will Rogers' daughter we

feel that she will display that same pluck that he always revealed in the pinches, and continue to carry on.

That evening, the sixteenth, the three women left Lakewood in a car with Bogart and Owen Davis for the drive to a small station near Waterville, twenty miles south. In New York they stayed one night, and by Tuesday, August 20 they were home on the ranch in Santa Monica, again in seclusion as they awaited the return of Will's body. Then would come the funeral.

Back at Lakewood, the theater's staff and directors were as strongly affected by Rogers' death as anyone, perhaps more so since they also witnessed the impact on his wife and daughter. But this was show business, and business was business. So despite what some people advised, and even insisted, *Ceiling Zero* would not be canceled. It would finish out its regular week's run, with those three more performances as scheduled, on Friday and Saturday.

Another actress—Hope Lauder, who'd had a supporting role in the original Broadway production, and who happened to be visiting Lakewood that week—jumped in for Mary, and that same evening the curtain opened again on *Ceiling Zero*, now everybody's big ticket. All were curious to hear the terrible sound of the play's two plane crashes over the loudspeaker that, as rumor declared and the papers strongly implied, had so shattered poor, vulnerable Mary.

Saturday's two performances, at two and eight p.m., were both standing-room only.

IF YOU WANT TO KNOW WHO WILL ROGERS WAS, what he meant to people then and to the life of the nation, there's one quick way. Have a look at a sampling of the countrywide explosion of newspaper coverage that announced his death. For a private citizen there'd never been anything like it. This was not just a loved show business celebrity who died. Here was one of those unique personalities who somehow work and charm their way deep into people's minds and hearts, into their view of daily, ordinary things, as well as their affections.

From Maine to California if there was one paper that didn't front-page the news, often in headlines of what editors used to call Second-Coming type, treating many angles of the story for days, it hasn't turned up yet. Here without comment are some front pages with interior stories from different papers that hit the streets on August 17, morning and afternoon editions—the news from Barrow came too late for the papers on the sixteenth. It's a very small sampling, of course. But even the more than fifty papers looked at for this study was a tiny portion of the amazing reality.

The South's
Standard
Newspaper

A. P. Service
United Press
N. A. N. A.

THE ATLANTA CONSTITUTION

The Daily Constitution Leads in Home Delivered, City, Trading Territory and Total Circulation

ONLY MORNING NEWSPAPER
PUBLISHED IN ATLANTA

Entered at Atlanta Postoffice
As Second-Class Mail Matter.

ATLANTA, GA., SATURDAY MORNING, AUGUST 17, 1935.

Single Copies: Daily, 5c; Sunday, 10c.
Daily and Sunday Weekly 20c; Weekly 5c.

VOL. LXVIII., No. 66.

POST AND ROGERS ARE CRUSHED TO DEATH AS ENGINE FAILS, PLANE DIVES SIXTY FEET

CHAIRMAN ADAMS AND ED L. ALMAND DUBBED INCAPABLE

In Special Presentment Jurors Charge Lack of Good Faith to Fulton Commission and Repeat Extravagance Accusation

JOHNSON CONTROL OF MAJORITY CITED

Commission Dominated by Edwin Johnson, Says Jury, Attributing Political Aims as His Motive.

Charging that Chairman C. R. Adams and Commissioner Ed L. Almand are incapable of handling county affairs in the best interests of the county, and that they are completely dominated by Commissioner Edwin F. Johnson, leader of the majority faction of the county commission, the July 14 last grand jury yesterday returned special presentments in its second special presentment that extravagance and recommended that an injunction be obtained to keep county expenditures within the budget.

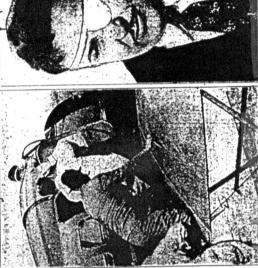

Friend, Humorist, Philosopher--Before Seattle Take-Off--'Round-World Record Breaker

Craft Constructed Of 2d-Hand Parts, Not Fully Licensed

Twice Forced Down by Fog and at a Loss for Directions, Pair Plummet Into Edge of River 15 Miles From Goal; Humorist Removed First But Rescuers Are Forced To Tear Ship Apart To Recover 'Round-the-WorldFlyer.

LINDBERGH SENDS SHIP TO ALASKA TO BRING BODIES BACK TO STATES

Natives at Outermost Post of Civilization Report Wiley's Specially-Built Engine Missed During Takeoff; Pilot Made Brave, Effort To Bank, But Ship Went Wild and Crashed.

(Copyright, 1935, by the Associated Press)

POINT BARROW, Alaska, Aug. 16.—(AP)—Death, on its tragic ...foot, overtook Will Rogers, peerless comedian, and Wiley Post, master aviator, as their rebuilt airplane faltered and fell into a shallow river last night near this bleak outpost of civilization.

They had just taken off for a trifling 10-minute flight, from their river position to Point Barrow. Sixty feet in the air the motor muffled.

The plane hurled over on the right wing as ...this world.

The lives of both the aviator and the wildfire and the chim...

k Times.

Company.

JST 17, 1935.

LATE CITY EDITION

WEATHER—Fair, continued warm
today; tomorrow cloudy, showers.
Temperatures, Yesterday—Max., 86; Min., 73

P　　TWO CENTS | In New York City. | THREE CENTS Within 200 Miles | FOUR CENTS Elsewhere Except In 7th and 8th Postal Zones.

ILL SPLITS DEMOCRATS; E HELD SURE

rty Schism Since Sentence' Marks Measure Debate.

BY 30 CLAIMED

tion Leaders Are t Despite Attacks constitutional.

THE NEW YORK TIMES.

TON, Aug. 16.—In the most serious party h has yet confronted dent Roosevelt's projstrial reform, the Guf'oal Bill was manoeuse leaders tonight into r final action on Mon-

al debate on the meased, they planned to rough the amending ow and adjourn before passage.

the vote on the Presind for the "death senutility holding comhe rank and file of the majority been so thoras on the merits of the ter measure, and leadrking overtime to make prediction that the bill by about thirty votes.

they conceded that the would be close, all said s had been obtained to age of the administrameasure. Their estiirty votes was verified an leaders.

ts" Oppose Measure.

of "unconstitutional," m," and , "regimentasome of those who have

WILL ROGERS, WILEY POST DIE IN AIRPLANE CRASH IN ALASKA; NATION SHOCKED BY TRAGEDY

Sergeant Morgan's Report of the Death Of Rogers and Post as Seen by Natives

Special to THE NEW YORK TIMES.

SEATTLE, Wash., Aug. 16.—The radio message sent by relays from Point Barrow, Alaska, to Seattle, in which Staff Sergeant Stanley R. Morgan informed the world of the tragic death of Will Rogers and Wiley Post, read as follows:

"Ten P. M. native runner reported plane crashed fifteen miles south of Barrow.

"Immediately hired fast launch, proceeded to scene.

"Found plane complete wreck, partly submerged, two feet water.

"Recovered body Rogers, then necessary tear plane apart extract body of Post from water.

"Brought bodies Barrow. Turned over Dr. Greist.

"Also salvaged personal effects, which am holding. Advise relatives and instruct this station fully as to procedure.

"Natives camping small river fifteen miles south here claim Post, Rogers landed and asked way to Barrow.

"Taking off, engine misfired on right bank while only fifty feet off water.

"Plane, out of control, crashed nose on, tearing right wing off and nosing over, forcing engine back through body of plane.

"Both apparently killed instantly.

"Both bodies bruised.

"Post's wrist watch broken, stopped 8:18 P. M."

The message was received by Colonel George E. Kumpe, in charge of the army signal corps headquarters here. It had been relayed through two radio stations and took about two hours to reach Seattle.

Sergeant Morgan won fame last Spring when he stayed at his post through a severe influenza epidemic while others, including his wife and 2-year-old son, Barrow, lay seriously ill. Sergeant Morgan and Dr. Henry W. Greist, the Presbyterian medical missionary, waged a bitter fight against the epidemic. While Dr. Greist ministered to the sick, Sergeant Morgan radioed for the aid which finally defeated the epidemic.

ETHIOPIANS OFFER　　CAPITAL SADDENED

10-MINUTE HOP THEIR LAST

Engine Fails on a Take-Off for Final 15 Miles to Point Barrow.

LANDED TO GET BEARINGS

Startled Eskimos See Huge Bird Plunge to River Bank From 50 Feet Above Water.

ONE RUNS 3 HOURS TO TELL

Humorist Revealed as Financing a Trip Around the World With Famous Pilot.

(Copyright, 1935, by The Associated Press.)

POINT BARROW, Alaska, Aug. 16.—Will Rogers, beloved humorist, and Wiley Post, master aviator, were crushed to death last night when a shiny, new airplane motor faltered and became an engine of tragedy near this outpost of civilization.

Both were killed when their red Arctic sky cruiser slipped and fell fifty feet head-on into a river bank. The 550-horse-power motor, driven back into the fuselage, snuffed out

enerosity Are Matche

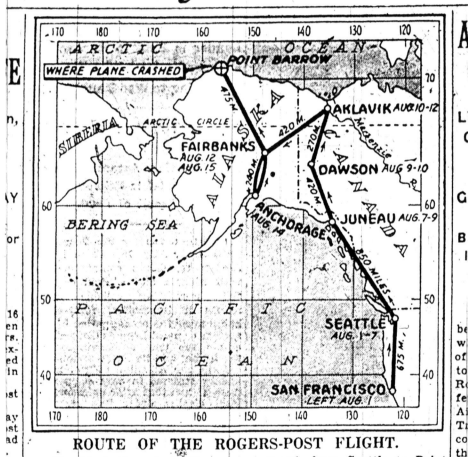

ROUTE OF THE ROGERS-POST FLIGHT.

The black line shows the areas covered, from Seattle to Point Barrow, on the fatal holiday jaunt.

ROGERS AND POST

girdling Winnie Mae, in which he twice circled the globe, after his attempts to span the continent in the substratosphere

EXTRA

TWO CENT

Post-Record

CITY NEWS

No. 12649 — Phone: TUcker 1121 — LOS ANGELES, FRIDAY, AUGUST 16, 1935 — In Two Sections—Section One

AIRPLANE CRASH KILLS WILL ROGERS, WILEY POST

Dead in Alaskan Wilds!   NOTED FLIERS PLUNGE TO

READ THE JOURNAL
For ALL The News of Vinita
And ALL of Her
Neighbors

Vinita Daily Journal

Make Vinita

LEASED UNITED PRESS & A.A. SERVICE

39TH YEAR—NO. 223   VINITA, OKLAHOMA, FRIDAY, AUGUST 16, 1935   PRICE FIVE CENTS

CRASH KILLS ROGERS-POST

PLANNING BOARD IS SELECTED FOR COUNTY PROJECTS

Huey Figures in Their Run-Off

'WEALTH TAX' BILL PASSED BY SENATE BY VOTE OF 57-23

TWO OKLAHOMANS KILLED IN ALASKA AT FIVE O'CLOCK THURSDAY ALASKA TIME

EXTRA

FIFTH EXTRA

Only Los Angeles Newspaper With All Leading News Services—Associated Press, International News, United Press, Dow-Jones

Los Angeles Evening HERALD Express

SPORTS COMPLETE N.Y. STOCKS

The Evening Herald and Express Covers Just Like Los Angeles

VOL. LXX   THREE CENTS   FRIDAY, AUGUST 16, 1935   THREE CENTS   NO. 123

WILL ROGERS AND POST KILLED IN AIR CRASH

ROOSEVELT VOICES GRIEF OF NATION

Tributes Swell to Avalanche as Shocked U.S. Hears of Air Tragedy

(By Associated Press)

The death of Will Rogers and Wiley Post shocked the United States and brought expressions of profound sympathy from all over the world.

Men high in the worlds of statecraft, aviation and the theater voiced their sorrow at the passing of these two pioneers in their respective fields.

President Roosevelt expressed the grief of the American people. Congress paused to pay an unusual tribute.

"I was shocked to hear of the tragedy which has taken Will Rogers Wiley Post from us," said President Roosevelt. "Will was an old friend of mine, a humorist and philosopher beloved by all. I had the pleasure of greeting Mr. Post on his return from his round-the-world flight. He leaves behind a splendid contribution to the science of aviation. Both were outstanding Americans and will be greatly missed."

Garner "Just Can't Talk."

Other expressions of grief, voiced in Congress and elsewhere, follow:

VICE PRESIDENT GARNER: "Two mighty good men have been lost to the world. I just can't talk about it."

HERBERT HOOVER: "In origin and accomplishment they were typically American, with their careers appealing to everyone appreciative of the pioneer spirit. They were great souls and I feel a sense of deep personal loss in their passing."

ALFRED E. SMITH: "The news comes as a distinct shock as they were two great Americans who will be missed by everybody."

THE PRINCE OF WALES, through his personal aid-de-camp, Maj. Sir John Aird—"The prince learns with deep regret the sad news of the untimely death of Mr. Will Rogers and Mr. Wiley Post."

WILL H. HAYS—"It does not take time to realize our loss. The intensity of this loss is as instantly grasped as the effect of the crash itself. He stood for everything that was right, never for anything that was wrong."

"Had Public's Ear."

SPEAKER BYRNS of the House of Representatives—"Will Rogers had the ear of the public as few in this country did. His death is a real loss and Post's is too. When I read Rogers was going on that long trip I told my wife 'I wish Will Rogers wouldn't do that.' I said he was liable to get killed."

CAPT. EDDIE RICKENBACKER, American war ace—"Both Rogers and Post have been pioneers with new equipment over uncharted skyways. Will Rogers was not a passenger but an adventurer with Wiley."

GENE BUCK, president of the American Society of Composers, Authors and Publishers—"I can hardly believe that Will Rogers' voice is stilled forever. I do not believe we will see his like again."

FRANK HAWKS, noted aviator—"America has lost a great person in Will Rogers and a great flyer in Wiley Post."

REPRESENTATIVE WILL ROGERS of Oklahoma—"Oklahoma has lost its two greatest sons."

MAYOR LA GUARDIA of New York—"Every good American will feel a personal loss in the sudden passing of these two beloved characters."

WILL ROGERS WON PRAISE OF WILSON

Talks Humorous and Illuminating, Said Late President

This a the 13th of a series of articles on the life of Will Rogers, the best loved American of his time.

BY MICHEL MOK
Copyright, 1935, by New York Post, Inc.

It was a president of the United States who discovered that Will Rogers was a good deal more than a lariat-swinging cowboy comedian. Woodrow Wilson was the first to call Mr. Rogers a humorist.

"His remarks," said the late war-time president, "are not only humorous but illuminating."

Mr. Wilson made this flattering comment while discussing Will's book "A Cowboy Philosopher on the Peace Conference" (1919). Here is a paragraph the president singled out as being particularly penetrating:

"It says here there are to be no more wars, and then there is a paragraph further down telling you where to get your ammunition in case there is one."

The esteem was mutual. That same year, 1919, Will told a friend:

"President Wilson is my best audience. I have played to him five times, and I always use lots of stuff about him. The one he afterward repeated as being a good one on him was just before we got into the war. I said:

"'Well, President Wilson will have it pretty easy now, as Germany is five notes behind.'"

Wise-Cracks Fail

"A Cowboy Philosopher at the Peace Conference" marked Will's debut as a writer. The little book did not make much of a hit with the public. A bruised, bleeding war-weary world was in no mood to listen to cracks about the peace covenant from a grinning Oklahoma plainsman.

But those whose business it is to buy and sell written words saw great future possibilities in the quasi-naive, studiously unlettered commentator from the west.

Publishers, editors, realized that Will was a coming American spokesman. They begged Rogers for his stuff. In the years that followed he could write anything he pleased, from any spot on earth where he happened to be.

WILL'S GAGS MADE COOLIDGE SMART

Imitated Nasal Drawl Too Well; Harding Was Also Irritated.

WASHINGTON, Aug. 16.—Some of the best gags Will Rogers ever uttered burned through the tough hides of Washington politicians.

That is why the capital for a score of years has been half angry although amused by the comedian who died in the crash of Wiley Post's new airplane.

Jaws rolling the inevitable gum, chin on hands, Rogers was a familiar figure in Senate and House press galleries. In the back galleries where reporters rest or work, he would impersonate this or that pompous gentleman who just had been speaking on the floor.

But representatives and congressmen could take it. Rogers' friction in Washington usually was with the White House. Presidents Harding and Coolidge, in turn, fell out with the Oklahoma cowboy whose boyish surprise and regret that he had caused annoyance to the chief executive caused many a chuckle among those who like to see the big fellows squirm a bit or who may have suspected Rogers was less sorry than he seemed that his satire had raised a blister on the presidential skin.

Imitated Coolidge.

Born mimic that he was, Rogers was tempted by Mr. Coolidge's peculiar nasal tones, and he imitated the president on the radio. It was an almost-perfect job—too perfect, Mr. Coolidge thought.

The New York Times took Rogers to task in an editorial, contending that the high office of president should be above the buffoonery of a comedian. Rogers answered by showing a telegram in which Coolidge gave him permission for the imitation. Coolidge, however, probably never dreamed that Will would do it so accurately.

Ike Hoover, White House usher who died about two years ago, relates in his book of presidential recollections that Mr. Coolidge was angry.

Never Invited Back.

"He sent a letter apologizing, but never got back into the president's good graces," Ike Hoover wrote. "Coolidge especially disliked the nasal tone adopted in imitating him."

remarked that Rogers had been a guest in the White House once, but if he was to be again some other president would have to do the inviting."

Rogers got a taste of the Coolidge punctuality on the occasion of that White House visit. It was in 1926. Rogers was invited for the night but his train was late and he arrived at the White House approximately one minute late for dinner.

Imitated Harding.

"The president and Mrs. Coolidge had just come down in the elevator on their way to the dining room," Ike Hoover recalled of this incident, "and were told that Mr. Rogers was

ROGERS AND POST LOST IN FOG AFTER WARNINGS; DIED IN REBUILT PLANE

OF UTILITIES BILL IS SEEN

Party Chiefs Think Measure Will Be Left Behind at This Session Unless There Is Speed.

ROOSEVELT MOVES TO HASTEN ADJOURNMENT

Calls Parley of Democratic Leaders for Sunday to Make Plans.

WASHINGTON, Aug. 16.—(AP)—

1935 DOOM — Rogers and Post Before Flight; Grandmother Grieves

MRS. GENE POST.

NEW MOTOR OF CRAFT WITH LIMITED LICENSE FALTERED AT 60 FEET

POINT BARROW, Alaska, Aug. 16.—Death, breaking through an Arctic fog, overtook Will Rogers, peerless comedian and Wiley Post, master aviator, as their rebuilt airplane leaped and fell into an icy little river last night near this lone outpost of civilization.

They had just taken off for a trailing ten-minute flight from their river position to Point Barrow. Sixty feet in the air the motor misfired. The plane banked over on its right wing.

It is said both the gentle master of the wisecrack and the champion aerial globe trotter were crushed out instantly as the impact drove the heavy motor back through the fuselage.

Used Second-Hand Parts.

It became known in Los Angeles that the multi-millioned airplane that carried Rogers and Post was assembled of second-hand parts and operating under a restricted government license.

At the Burbank (Cal.) plant where the ship was assembled under Post's direction it was said that although the craft had a new 550-horse power motor, it was not considered a new type of ship.

Aviation men said the fuselage was taken from a plane that had ground-looped and damaged its wings. The wings of the Post plane, they said, were taken from a second ship.

The bodies rested tonight in the Presbyterian Mission ware house here, in he flown to Fairbanks by the flying friends of both men, Pilot Joe Crosson. Flying from Fairbanks, reached Point Barrow tonight.

DALLAS, Tex., Aug. 16.—(AP)— Rogers and Post had landed on the river where the Arctic fog hung thin over the uncertain of their bearings on a 500-mile flight from Fairbanks to Point Barrow.

Post and Rogers took off in the face of a report that the was a dense fog along the route and the thermometer registered 45 degrees.

First Photo—Where Rogers and Post Met Death

Copyright, 1935, Associated Press WIREPHOTO.

Flown thousands of miles from Point Barrow to San Francisco at a cost of $1,700, The Post this morning, through the facilities of Wirephoto, which flashed the photograph across the 3,000 miles from the coast, is able to give Washington the first pictures of the actual crash of the Rogers-Post plane in Alaska on Thursday night.

Riots Renewed As Dr. Schacht Cautions Nazis

Trouble Spreads as Bank President Tells How It Hurts Germany.

By the United Press.

Funeral Plane Stops Overnight In Vancouver on Seattle Flight

Guard Watches Bodies of Post and Rogers as Crosson Rests for Third Stage of 3,600-Mile Journey; Crowds Wait at Airport.

By the Associated Press.

——— 18. The bodies of Will Rogers and Wiley Post

---

2 Ocean Liners Collide in Fog; 6 Dead, 5 Hurt

Sailors Crushed in Bunks of Cruise Boat in Crash Off Irish Coast.

By the Associated Press.

Liverpool, Aug. 18.—Six seamen

New York World-Telegram

VOL. 68—NO. 40.—IN TWO SECTIONS—SECTION ONE. NEW YORK, FRIDAY, AUGUST 16, 1935. PRICE THREE CENTS.

SPORTS
7TH RACE RESULTS
BOX SCORES

WILL ROGERS AND POST DIE AS PLANE CRASHES

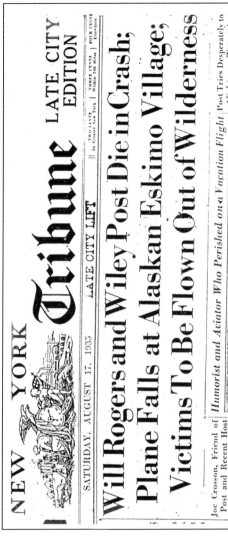

NEW YORK

New York Tribune

LATE CITY EDITION

LATE CITY LIFE

SATURDAY, AUGUST 17, 1935.

Will Rogers and Wiley Post Die in Crash; Plane Falls at Alaskan Eskimo Village; Victims To Be Flown Out of Wilderness

Humorist and Aviator Who Perished on a Vacation Flight

Joe Crosson, Friend of Post and Recent Host to Both, Arrives at the Scene in Funeral Plane

Post Tries Desperately to Alight on Water, but Plunges on Riverbank, a Few Feet From Safety

Begins as Cowboy and
Dies World Renowned

Will Rogers, Victim of Plane Tragedy, Had Only to Smile to Make the World Laugh; He Was Master of the "Wise-crack"

Will Rogers was given the imposing name of William Penn Adair Rogers but everybody called him Will. He was a cowboy, humorist, writer, lecturer, philosopher, polo player, world traveler and flyer, but he went up in the air only as a passenger.

He was born at Oolagah, Indian Territory, November 4, 1879, but he called Claremore, Okla., his "home town" and he was a legal resident of Oklahoma although he spent most of his time at his ranch between Beverly Hills and Santa Monica, California.

He had Indian blood in his veins and was proud of it. One of his best wisecracks was based upon this ancestry as he said that his ancestry did not come over on the Mayflower, but they met the boat.

WILL ROGERS

His education came he said, by easy stages. "I studied the fourth reader for ten years" he told an interviewer, but he was a "kidder" on and off the stage and many of his boasts of being "ignerant" could be taken with a grain of salt.

After he left the fourth reader behind him he went through the Willow Hassell school at Neosho, Mo., and Kemper Military Academy at Booneville and if he did not make a remarkable record for scholarship he did not fail.

His mother wanted him to become a Methodist minister but Will had learned to ride a horse and throw a rope on his father's ranch so he went back to the range. Then starting with medicine shows and carnivals he went on along the road that finally brought him to the very top of his profession as an actor. A rancher, Zach Mulhall, organized a wild west show and Will joined it, finally reaching New York.

There is a tradition that he first attracted public notice on a large scale when he lassoed a wild steer that broke loose at Madison Square Garden and was about to dash through the crowd.

Certainly shortly after his first appearance at "the garden" he was on the vaudeville stage. Charley Mack of Moran and Mack told of Will's initial efforts in vaudeville. He was pretty bad said Mack and grew discouraged. He talked it over with Charley.

"Where are you going?" asked Mack.

"Back to Oklahoma."

"Been fired yet?"

"The manager said I was pretty punk."

"Yeh, you're all of that; but has he actually told you that you are fired?"

"Well, no."

"Don't quit till he tells you; maybe you can stick it out to Saturday night. That will be three days' more pay."

Before the week was out, Will happened to make a wise crack about something he saw in a newspaper, an observation shyly delivered of something that struck his fancy. The audience laughed. Rogers tried some other joshing remarks, and was "made."

It was a short step to Hammerstein's Roof at $150 a week and then he spent six years as the star of Ziegfeld's Follies.

He ventured into motion pictures but failed to score the success expected. The silent screen gave the comedian no chance to convulse his audiences with his homely observations rendered in a drawl that only Rogers knew. But when talking pictures appeared, Rogers became a boxoffice riot and thereafter the legitimate theater saw little of him.

When his friend, Fred Stone, was injured in an airplane accident, in 1929, just before he was to open a new play in New York, Rogers rushed across the continent, took the role "for old Fred" and scored another hit.

He continued, however, to go on "lecture tours" packing great crowds into theaters, auditoriums, schoolhouses and churches. He raised a small fortune for the drought sufferers in 1930, and in his quiet way gave thousands of dollars of his private fortune to charity.

His wealth was estimated by his friends at several million dollars and he carried life insurance of approximately $1,000,000. He never

d Times-Dispatch

Phone Your
WANT AD
Before 5 o'Clock Today
DIAL 3-3431

Richmond, Virginia, Saturday, August 17, 1935   Dial 3-3431 Calls The Times-Dispatch   Three Cents

Italy Offered New African Concessions

Mussolini, However, Is Silent on What He Wants in Ethiopia as 3 Powers Confer

Problem 'Dumped' In Il Duce's Lap

Roman Press Bars Any Compromise; Lloyds' Rates on War Rise

PARIS, Aug. 16.— [—Ethiopia] of-f[ ], Italy econom[ic] concessions [ ], but Mussolini's unwillingness to [ ] France and England exactly what [ ] wants baked effort to avert a [ ]

In a message to the [Emperor] concerning the [ ] kingdom [ ]m[ ] he would [ ] accept a military occupation.

His offer climaxed long deliberation by Premier Pierre Laval of [ ], Anthony Eden of Great Britain, and Baron Pompeo Aloisi of Italy [ ] talks formally were opened.

Statement Withheld

A British spokesman said Aloisi was [ ] for a [ ] France statement of [ ] Mussolini wants. He declined to [ ] it, but instead quit the meeting and telephoned Il Duce. "This now lap the whole thing has now been dumped," the spokesman asserted.

Through his minister to Paris Haile [Selassie] laid the following proposal before the three powers:

(1) A guarantee of the security of the Italian colonies of Somaliland and Eritrea and of the security of Italians living in Ethiopia.

(2) The granting to Italy of economic facilities for mining, road-building and railway operations in Ethiopia.

(3) The possibility of even more extensive agricultural concessions to [ ]

Treaties Are Analyzed

After a full meeting of all three delegations, Laval announced the day had been devoted to analyzing diplomatic documents, presumably treaties involved in the dispute, and that further discussions would be held tomorrow.

Aloisi left Laval and Eden with a perfunctory nod, said a "Bon soir good night" as soon as the meeting was over. Eden remained while Laval read the communique.

The British spokesman said: "The British and French who, the Italians to state real claim against Ethiopia. "We feel if the Italians state their claim it will be found a very large part of them will be met freely by Ethiopia. In fact, Italy probably can attain a very large part of what she wants while retaining the friendship of Ethiopia, avoiding a breach with the French and British governments and the League of Nations, and without embarking on a very doubtful adventure."

Rogers, Post Killed in Crash Of Plane in Northern Alaska; Tragedy Shocks Whole World

Died When Motor Failed in Alaskan Wilds

—Associated Press Photo.
Wiley Post

—Associated Press Photo.
Will Rogers

Britain Calls Naval Parley For October

Diplomatists Dubious Over Five Power Conference Due to World Affairs

LONDON, Aug. 16.— (AP)—Great Britain called a preliminary naval conference today for October but diplomatic circles were dubious over the prospect.

These circles felt the trend of the Italo-Ethiopian dispute and the general naval situation made it uncertain whether the five powers could get together. If they do, they will seek a limitation treaty replacing those expiring at the end of 1936.

Feels U. S. Should Call Parley

Those invited are the proposed signatories of a new Washington

City and State Join Nation In Tribute to Rogers, Post

Peery Calls Humorist 'Influence for Good'; Famed Pair's Visits to Richmond Recalled

Expressions of personal loss sprang spontaneously to the lips of Governor Peery and Virginians in all walks of life yesterday as the news of the death of Will Rogers and his friend, Wiley Post, round-the-world flyer, was flashed from Alaska.

Thousands of Richmonders had seen Will Rogers on one or more of the many visits here by the homespun philosopher and thousands more had read his daily and Sunday articles in The Times-Dispatch and had seen the movies in which he was starred. Wiley Post, too, was acquainted here. He had been a guest of honor January 21, 1934 at a dinner when he piloted Keith Morgan of the Warm Springs Foundation in preparation for the nation-wide celebration of President Roosevelt's birthday.

"Will Rogers was a fine influence

New Motor Fails on Takeoff After Halt in Fog; Ship Falls 60 Feet Into River

Death Ends Flight 15 Miles From Goal

Bodies Being Flown To Civilization By Pilot Joe Crosson of Regular Air Line

Wife Begged Rogers Not to Make Flight

BURBANK, CAL., Aug. 16.—(AP)—"Don't go Will. Please don't go."

This was the plea of Mrs. Will Rogers when she and their son, Will Jr., were at the Union Air Terminal to see him off as he took an airliner to meet Wiley Post in Seattle, terminal attendants recalled today.

They said she pointed to the dangers of flying over icy wastes in Alaska and Siberia and begged him not to make the trip.

Copyright, 1935, By The AP

POINT BARROW, ALASKA, Aug. 16—Death, grim stalker through an Arctic fog, overtook Will Rogers, peerless comedian, and Wiley Post, master aviator, as their rebuilt airplane faltered and fell into an icy little river last night near this bleak outpost of civilization.

They had just taken off for a trifling 10-minute flight from their river position to Point Barrow. Sixty feet in the air the motor misfired. The plane heeled over on its right wing and plunged to the ground.

The lives of both the gentle master aerial globe trotter were crushed out instantly as the impact drove the heavy motor back through the fuselage.

Bodies Flown Out

Tonight, Pilot Joe Crosson of the Alaska Airways was returning to Fairbanks, Alaska, with their bodies.

The Coast Guard at Washington, D. C., was informed that Crosson arrived at Point Barrow, Alaska, at 4 P. M., Eastern Standard Time.

He planned to proceed from Fairbanks to Juneau, the Coast Guard was informed.

Dr. Henry W. Greist, medical missionary, said the rescue party reported the plane debris was readily removed as it was torn and broken to

Whole World Is Shocked By Plane Tragedy

Roosevelt Leads U. S. in Paying Tribute to Rogers,

THIS FROZEN LAND

is where Will Rogers and Wiley Post met death when their plane crashed Thursday night. These photographs of Point Barrow, Alaska, are from the collection of Robert H. Sayre, Denver mining engineer, who spent several weeks this summer in the Point Barrow region. They were taken by Noel Wien, Fairbanks, Alaska, operator of an airplane service.

The town of Point Barrow, northermost settlement on the American contine. the air.

Another view of Point Barrow, taken from Wien's plane, showing how the settlement is surrounded by arctic steppes and ice floes.

Desolate Spot Claimed Lives of Post and Rogers

By Associated Press

SEATTLE — The place where Wiley Post and Will Rogers met death in an airplane crash Thursday night was described by Andy Bahr, noted reindeer driver, as "one of the most desolate places in the world."

Bahr won fame for his five-year trek with a herd of reindeer from Barrow across the tundra to the Mackenzie River basin to feed Canadian Eskimos. The trek ended this spring.

Bahr, who lives here and is familiar with the region south of Point Barrow, described it as mostly tundra, disagreeable even at this time of year and terribly stormy in winter.

"It's a bad country," he said. "It's horrible to die anywhere, but the place where Rogers and Post were killed is a lonely, miserable spot."

Ralph Lomen, vice president of the Lomen Reindeer Corporation, and known as "the reindeer king of Alaska," for whom Bahr made his historic trek, also knows the region well.

"Post and Rogers already had crossed the Endicott Mountain range and were over a flat, desolate country, with low, rolling hills," he said. "The whole coast there is flat and barren."

ROGERS SHUNNED FILMLAND FRILLS

His Dressing Room Looked Like Third Floor Back in Tenement.

HOLLYWOOD, Aug. 17.—(AP).—
The door of Will Rogers' dressing room at his movie studio was opened and closed, for the last time today. It isn't much of a dressing room.

Put it in a tenement house, on the third floor back, with a view of the "elevated," and it would be typical. Three about right.

The man door never tion picture million dol think so, room.

The big r tric lights.

Covere

It has fly because th door is wor bulbs are b newsapers tables.

What wo is covered

Rogers Gave an Epitaph For Gravestone in 1930

By The Associated Press.
BOSTON, Aug. 16.—The death of Will Rogers recalled remarks he made in a speech here in 1930 concerning the epitaph to be placed on his grave.

"When I die, my epitaph, or whatever you call those signs on gravestones, is going to read: 'I joke about every prominent man of my time, but I never met a man I didn't like.'

"I am proud of that," Mr. Rogers added. "I can hardly be carved. around to bly find me reading it."

Country Mourns for Rogers As Its Homespun Philosopher

Comedian of Stage, Screen and Radio Carried His Simplicity of Livi——
Hearers in

Will Rogers, Oklahoma cowbe star comedian of stage, screen ar radio and America's nearest ap he never wanted to be taken ac ously while alive and probably r

---

Whole World Is Shocked By Plane Tragedy

Roosevelt Leads U. S. in Paying Tribute to Rogers, Post: Congress Pauses

NEW YORK, Aug. 16—(Æ)—The death of Will Rogers and Wiley Post shocked the United States and brought expressions of profound sympathy from all over the world.

Men high i the theatre v Roos President grief of the A gress paused moving tribut dead.

"I was shoc dy which ha Wiley Post fi oosevelt. "W ine, a humo ved by all. eeting Mr. y round-the hind a sple

---

Tragedy News Causes Tears In Hollywood

There Rogers Had Characteristically Told His Faith in Post.

By the United Press.
Hollywood, Aug. 16. — Will Rogers left here for the Alaska flying adventure in which he died with an expression of faith in his pilot, Wiley Post.

"I don't know much about air— but if Wiley is the pilot I to know much," Will olony read accounts of with universal sorrow. ly humor touched all— ents and Kings to the piler—so tonight his prop boys, extra girls, hters.

Stone Weeps.

e, Rogers' closest per— wept. has lost a great man lost my best friend."

ke, widow of Flo Zeig— scovered" Rogers, said; e kindest man in ad known him for so Just starting out in the my husband died Will other to me."

Will's airplane crash in pt Hollywood boule— ne was sobered. Many

stories of the kindly, Oklahoman's homely

lot roadways, stage— stories of the actor— ld miss an important gagement to take a or stage technicians to shocking sedate old pearing in overalls.

With Workmen.

he wouldn't live at a camp with workmen nds.

on every Will Rogers oat which he used to ng. ncluded:

Mille—"What can any— in one of the greatest in the world is taken

---

Rogers' Last Wisecracks Kept Colonists Roaring

BY ARVILLE SCHALEBEN
(Copyright, 1935, by N. A. N. A. Inc.)
PALMER, Alas., Aug. 14.—Will ped into the Matanuska 3:15 p. m. Wednesday ecrack on his lips. He the colony "fine, fine minute examination and h a departing wisecrack the wake of the mono-

view this correspondent e noted humorist in his see his face, for it was 24 hours later that Wiley Post were killed plane crashed a few d Post flew from Fair— ed over the field where here, and seemed so te when Chief Pilot Joe dmit the airport was too a big job. "That McLean. as a most famous flyers, back here in a small

a getting tired of travel— as comforted He fait he way out Post kept a eye alert and because what McLean dropped

his homely and in using observations. But ng pictures appeared ame a box-office hit and time on the legitimate little of him. His most worthy stage appearance when he rushed across it to take the part of his lend, Fred Stone, in a ction. An airplane ac— forced Stone to with— the cast. itself, although he never pilot a plane, was a He crossed the United

In over the construction ca land. "That field looks rough," he said.

Administrator Hunt, Co-Ordinator Carr of the transient workers swarm before ship ac Mr. R "WS will ya "I can port at "Wh pushin, in get Claram Oklaho That 1Go

WH
Movies Turned Editor Mailion Bygone Finance Mu. Marine Radio

Rogers Twice Escaped Death in Plane Crashes

Special to THE NEW YORK TIMES.
LOS ANGELES, Aug. 16.—Saddened by the loss of one of the film colony's most popular members, friends of Will Rogers recalled today that he twice escaped death in the air.

On June 6, 1928, a passenger plane in which he was crossing the continent nosed over while landing at Las Vegas, Nev. Rogers, shaken but unhurt, came out with:

"I just started for the Republican convention at Kansas City. Serves me right for not going to the Democratic convention instead."

His second escape occurred on the same trip, when another plane in which he was riding landed hard and smashed its undercarriage.

ROGERS AND POST HONORED ABROAD

Leaders in London Join Press in Paying Tribute to the Actor and Aviator.

SOVIET OFFICIALS SHOCKED

Udet, German Ace, Calls Flier Greatest of His Time and Real Pioneer of Air.

Special Cable to THE NEW YORK TIMES.
LONDON, Aug. 16.—The popularity which Will Rogers enjoyed in Great Britain may be measured to some extent by the way the news of his death and that of his companion

Stockton DAILY Record HOME EDITION

THE WEATHER
SAN JOAQUIN VALLEY—Fair tonight and
Saturday; slowly rising temperature.
SAN FRANCISCO BAY REGION—Fair and
mild tonight and Saturday; occasional fog near
coast.
TEMPERATURE—Yesterday: High 81,
low 51. This morning: Low 51.

Today's Market and Financial Review   New York and San Francisco Quotations

VOL. LXXXI   Twenty-Two Pages   STOCKTON, SAN JOAQUIN COUNTY, CALIFORNIA—FRIDAY, AUGUST 16, 1935.   No. 111

WILL ROGERS, WILEY POST KILLED IN AIRPLANE CRASH

Two Famous America...

COMPLETE STATE EDITION
★★★★★

STOCK MARKET
CLOSING PRICES

ST. LOUIS STAR-TIMES

28 PAGES   PRICE THREE CENTS

VOL 49—NO 271   ST. LOUIS, SATURDAY, AUGUST 17, 1935.

WILL ROGERS AND WILEY POST KILLED

...rist and Plane in Which They Crashed

NOTED HUMORIST AND ROUND-WORLD FLYER DIE IN ALASKAN CRASH

Plane Plunges 50 Feet Into Stream as
Motor Misses Fire in Take-Off 15
Miles South of Point Barrow—
Bodies Recovered by Army Man—
Wreckage Partly Submerged.

Star-Times 18 Minutes Ahead

...R JEALOUS OF RIVALS MIND   Story on Page 3

...LY MIRROR **FINAL**

New York... August 17, 1935

...ROGERS.
...ST DIE
...CRASH

Death
Came...

DAILY ⚫ NEWS **FINAL**

NEW YORK'S PICTURE NEWSPAPER

Daily — 1,525,000
Sunday — 2,400,000

26 Pages   New York, Saturday, August 17, 1935.   2 Cents

VOL 17. No. 42

U.S. MOURNS ROGERS, POST

—Story on Page 3

...n Plane

EXTRA

WEATHER

WISCONSIN NEWS
EVENING EDITION

From DALY 3300   MILWAUKEE, FRIDAY, AUGUST 16, 1935   Price 3 Cents

ROGERS, POST DIE IN CRASH

Plane Falls in Wilds of Alaska

11

PAIN MARRING her beautiful features, Lillian Crosson stood listening anxiously at the closed door. Never had she seen her husband so upset, so emotionally distraught.

That Joe, with all his rugged strength and silent independence, was a very sensitive man, she knew well. His quick, open response to suffering or any trying situation involving family or friends no longer surprised her. This was different. The gut-wrenching news that reached them early that morning—a six o'clock phone call from the office of Pacific Alaska Airlines—about the crack-up at Barrow and the deaths of Wiley and Will had bowled him over as if he'd been clubbed from behind. At the moment in their Fairbanks apartment he was locked in the bathroom, and from the sounds coming from the small room, he was throwing up.

The shaken Lillian turned, crossed the room and sat on the couch, trembling hands covering her tear-stained face.

At the sound of an opening door she looked up to see Joe coming toward her, pale and slumped. He sat beside her and reached for her hand. "Why did I let him go?" he mumbled. "I should have been able to talk him out of it, to make him see. All he had to do was wait!"

"Joe, don't . . . it wasn't—"

"I stood there and waved to them as he began to taxi. I think I was even smiling. You hear me, Lil, I waved and smiled when they took off. Knowing the chance he was taking! If I'd been more—"

"Stop, Joe! Please stop. You know you can't—"

"'Go on up there,' I said to them. 'You shouldn't miss Barrow,' I said. I can hear myself—"

"Will *wanted* to go. It wasn't you. Remember how he talked about going to the top of the world? And that Brower, he was a good part of it."

"I should have guessed he wouldn't call me from Harding before he left. I almost *knew* he wouldn't call. And I just stood there . . ." He got up, went to the telephone on a side table, and dialed. "Chuck? Listen. Get that number three Fairchild ready. The one with the floats. Take out the five rearmost seats. Full tanks, and put those cans of extra gas aboard. Call Bob Gleason and tell him that I need him to go with me. Where? Barrow."

He hung up and was heading for the bedroom when Lillian jumped up from the couch. "Did you say Barrow? You're going to Barrow?"

"Yes." From the closet he pulled a bag and began stuffing it with clothes and other items.

"Joe, you can't! What for?"

"Bring them home. They have to come home, don't they? I'll bring them home."

"Wait, Joe, wait. Let somebody else . . . you know you're too upset to fly now, and in a place like that! Why must it be today . . . why not—"

"It's all right, Lil. I'll have Bob with me as radio man, I won't be alone. Lil, I know the route like the back of my hand. Don't worry."

He went to the hall closet to gather his flying gear. As soon as he left the room Lillian picked up the phone and called the airfield. "Chuck, it's me, Lillian. Joe wants the weather at Barrow." She listened a few seconds, said "thanks," hung up, and followed Joe into the hall. "It's fogged in, Joe, just like yesterday, Chuck says just as bad. You *can't* go today. It's the same as yesterday, and you told Wiley—"

"Yes, but I know the way, the routes and where to land, if I have to, and Wiley didn't. I'll be heading for Barrow on a straight line from here, going westerly. The fog is mostly to the east."

"*Straight* from here to Barrow? But I heard you tell Wiley he'd have to follow the angle, go north from here and at the coast turn west and feel along for Barrow. That's the way you always went, isn't it? Why—"

"Sometimes straight is better. Could you put on some coffee? I want to leave for the field in a half hour. Have to stop on the way to pick up Bob. I'll take a thermos with me too."

A half hour later Joe donned his heavy jacket, picked up his bags, and went to the front door. "Be back tomorrow afternoon," he called over his shoulder. "Don't worry."

At the door stood Lillian, wrapped in her own heavy overcoat and fur hat. "I'm going to the field with you," she said, opening the door and walking out ahead of him. "The lady from upstairs is watching the kids."

Taking out the passenger seats in the airplane didn't require too much labor, and the gassing up went rapidly, so the plane was ready well before noon. There were an extra sixty gallons on board—twelve five-gallon cans. Compared to the line's flagship, a Lockheed Electra, the Fairchild had a shorter range. But for the five-hundred-mile trip to Barrow it was perfectly OK and would be more manageable landing on the Barrow lagoon than the bigger Lockheed. He'd use the Lockheed later, he decided, for the thousand-mile leg from Fairbanks to Seattle.

In the airfield's radio room, kissing Joe good-bye, Lillian refused to go home. What was the use, she scolded, did Joe think she'd be able to sleep or eat or anything while he was in the air over that awful Brooks Range, and feeling the way he did? She'd spend the night and next morning right here near the wireless. Bob would stay in touch with the field, and she'd *know* what was happening instead of brooding herself into a headache at home.

While they were still readying the plane a familiar face walked up to Crosson and asked if he had a minute. Sure, Murray, said Crosson, recognizing him. The man was Murray Hall, Alaskan agent for the U.S. Air Commerce Bureau. He'd been asked to look into the crash. Not to uncover or assign blame, if any, but to find its causes, helping assure air safety in future, although such an investigation was not usually done with private aircraft. As the bureau later admitted, the interest this time "was occasioned by the prominence of the pilot and passenger."

He'd like to inspect the wreck himself, said Hall, but at the moment he had no way of getting to Barrow. The Bureau plane he had at his disposal just then was much too light and short-range for such a trip and was on wheels. Did Joe have room for him?

Sorry, replied Crosson. The Fairchild was rated for six passengers. He'd have himself and Bob Gleason, and about four hundred pounds of extra gas aboard. He didn't want to chance an overload, especially if the weather went bad on him. Anyway, if he did take Hall, the agent would have to find his own way back, since he'd have the two bodies aboard and more extra gas. Sorry.

Hall said he understood, adding that if Joe himself had a good look at the wreck he'd see as much or more than anybody else, Hall would be satisfied with that, a written report by Joe.

"Here," he added, handing Crosson a telegram. "It's a later wire from Morgan. Has some detail about the crash. Not much, though."

Crosson took the piece of paper and put it in his pocket. "Send Morgan a wire that we're coming," he instructed the operator.

It was just after eleven o'clock in the morning when the Fairchild lifted off and headed north. After some seven hours of flying, mostly through nasty weather and including a stop on a remote lake to refuel, it touched down safely on the Barrow lagoon before the eyes of a large crowd. It had been far from an easy flight. Fifty years later, Gleason could still remember—and admit—that for the first time in an airplane he'd been "scared" (coming back especially, he said), when they'd gone roaring over and through those mountain passes. To find those not blocked by heavy, rolling fog, Joe had to fly into, then back out of, several before he succeeded. "Joe was trying to do too much, too fast," recalled Gleason, "trying a little too hard," driven by his grief over the two men's deaths, and what he'd convinced himself was his own failure to stop them.

First to greet the two as they stepped ashore in Barrow was Charlie Brower, acting in his role as U.S. Commissioner. Then Daugherty, Morgan, and Greist offered their hands. All four knew Crosson well from his previous visits.

"It's terrible, Joe, terrible," offered Brower. "I don't know what to say . . . to think that they were coming here because of me . . . let's go over to my place."

"Where are they? I'd like to see them."

"At my place. Have you decided what you want to do? You'll stay till tomorrow, I guess, and leave in the morning."

"Don't know yet. First I'd like to see them," said Crosson.

"You'll want to go out to Walakpa, I suppose. You'll want to have a look at the crash site."

"Yeah. First let's see them. Come on." To Gleason, Crosson suggested, "Bob, you better stay here with the wireless in case something comes up. I'll have a hot meal sent out."

The walk to Brower's house, on hard-trodden snow through the eastern end of the village, took some fifteen minutes. As they went, the other four and a crowd of silent Eskimos followed. "Here," said Brower, turning into his sprawling property and halting before one of the sheds standing opposite his house. "They're in here. But wait a minute, Joe. Why not rest up some first? Come in the house. We'll get some coffee."

"No. Open the shed." The look on Crosson's face had turned dark and grim.

Brower took out a key, unlocked the door and pulled it open. "Just you and me," ordered Crosson. "Everyone else stays out."

In the shed's center stood a broad table. Stretched on it side by side under a large canvas covering lay two bodies. Carefully Brower lifted off the canvas, revealing two bulky sleeping bags.

"Which one's Wiley?" asked Crosson with a sudden catch in his voice, his eyes darting from onc bag to the other.

Brower pointed.

"Let me see him. His face."

Brower took the sleeping bag zipper, pulled it down, and spread the bag's edges. Post's face showed no injury, looking relaxed, natural, at peace. Both eyes were closed, and there was no eye patch.

"You *had* to go!" burst out Crosson. "I told you not to go! Dammit, I *told* you!"

"Easy, Joe," said Brower, taking hold of Crosson's arm.

"Let me see Will."

Brower uncovered Rogers' face. Like Post's, it seemed at peace, though there were a few cuts and bruises that couldn't be hidden.

For some minutes Crosson stood staring at the two impassive faces, his stern glance shifting back and forth from one to the other. "God!" he muttered softly, then turned and walked out the door.

In the house, Brower's Eskimo wife had the table set and coffee ready. All five men, including Morgan, Daugherty, and Greist, sat talking. After he'd had a little rest, said Crosson, a couple of hours sleep, he'd go out to Walakpa to see the wreck. The government's Air Commerce Bureau at Fairbanks, he explained, wanted a detailed inspection. He wanted one, too.

"Anybody know exactly when it happened, the crash?" he asked, glancing around the table. "Has the time been fixed?"

"Seven-thirty, within a half hour on either side," replied Morgan. "Clair—the Eskimo runner—got to Frank's house at ten. He said he'd left the wreck site about two hours before. That makes it about eight o'clock. But he didn't start running for Barrow until some time after the crash, fifteen or twenty minutes after, or more. First he stood there shouting to the plane, then he thought about going out to it but concluded that the men must be dead and he wasn't sure that it might not explode or erupt in fire—the smell of gasoline was all around. Then he stopped in his tent to change his heavy boots for lighter mukluks, put on a thinner parka, then tried going with a canoe along the coast but gave it up because of the ice."

"Is he still here? Can I talk to him?"

"Name's Clair Okpeaha," said Brower. "Understands English and can speak it enough, though broken." He turned to his wife and said something in Inuit. She took off her apron, put on a coat, and went out.

Before Joe went to Walakpa, suggested Sergeant Morgan, maybe he'd like to see some pictures of the wreck, photographs. He'd developed the film soon after getting back from the crash site. Took a dozen good shots from different angles. They'd show him what to expect. Charlie's son Dave took some too, also Frank.

He hadn't thought of photos, admitted Crosson. Yes, he'd like very much to see them. Getting up, Morgan said it'd take him a few minutes to get them. He'd be right back.

While they waited, Crosson took out the telegram about the crash given him by Hall in Fairbanks. Based on Okpeaha's brief eyewitness description of the crash, it had little in the way of detail: "Taking off engine misfired on right bank while only fifty feet off water stop plane out of control crashed nose on tearing right wing off and nosing over forcing engine back through body of plane."

When Brower's wife returned she had Okpeaha in tow. At the table the men made room for him to sit and Brower introduced him to Crosson. "Tell me, Clair," he asked, "how close were you to the plane when it took off?"

"Lot close. Plane go slow down lagoon. Turn round come back fast. Go up. Me close forty feet."

"Did it take off at a steep angle or gradual?"

Okpeaha looked puzzled. Crosson lifted a hand. "Like this . . . or like this?"

"This." Okpeaha's hand traced a sharp rise.

"How high go up? Little high? Way up?"

"Maybe little high. Fifty, sixty fathom."

"Fathoms? You mean hundred feet? Two hundred?"

Okpeaha nodded. "I think more than hundred."

"When the engine stopped was plane high up? Two hundred?"

"Maybe."

"Was it a complete stop? I mean all stop, or little stop?"

"All stop. First little stop"—Okpeaha coughed—"then all stop."

"Then what happened? Plane fall down? Straight down? Or with a turn. Like this or like this."

Okpeaha raised his hand, showing a sharp swing to the right as it descended. "Plane crash. Blow up. Boom!"

"Blow up? How do you mean, blow up? What did it *look* like when it blew up?"

"Boom! Fire jump up high. Big smoke. White smoke. Steam maybe. Black smoke—"

"Fire? There was fire?"

"Much fire. Big fire. High."

"Where? The engine?"

"Engine. Little other place."

Crosson turned to look at Morgan and Daugherty. "Is there evidence of fire? Anywhere? In the cabin?"

"Not inside," replied Daugherty. "Only on a few scattered pieces we found in the water."

"Probably from the cockpit," added Morgan. "Also the engine cowling and such. Blistered metal and some bits of charred wood."

Crosson turned back to Okpeaha. "When you first see plane. Where was it?"

"First hear motor. I look. No see. Look more. No see. Motor go this way then go this way. I look that way to beach. See plane come down from fog over beach ice. Fly lagoon. Come down. Stop."

"How long did you hear it overhead *before* it came down? Many minutes? You hear, no see, for long time?"

"Not long time."

"Five minutes?" Crosson held up a hand with the fingers spread. Okpeaha held up both hands with all the fingers spread.

"When you *first* see plane, where was it? Barrow way? Or other way, Wainwright way?"

"Barrow."

"The plane landed first and the men talked to you. How long was it on the ground before it took off again? When the men got out, did they talk a lot—talk much or little? Did they walk around?"

"Mans talk much. Walk little. Big man say what I hunt. I tell seal, walrus, sometime caribou, sometime whale. On ground not long."

"Ten minutes? Twenty minutes?"

"Yes."

"Did the big man say anything else, talk more?"

"He say where seal, where walrus. I say out there, on ice." He pointed to the ocean. "He say I hunt polar bear? Sometime I say. Not much. Bear too big and hard find. I say sometime bear hunt me! Big man laugh."

"The other man, the man with the cover on his eye. Did he talk?"

"Not talk much. Look at plane."

Crosson turned to Brower. "Charlie, I want this to be clear. Ask Clair if the plane's right turn, the banking turn on the descent, started before the engine failed, or after. Or at the same time, or what. Tell him to picture it in his mind first."

Brower spoke several sentences in Inuit and listened as Okpeaha replied. "He thinks before. But he doesn't sound too sure. Could've been at the same time."

"Or after? Ask him."

Brower's question was short. Okpeaha hunched his shoulders and nodded yes. "Maybe after," said Brower.

"These are all good pictures," interrupted Sergeant Morgan as he came into the room brandishing an envelope. "Sharp and clear. Lots of detail." Taking the photos out of the envelope, he handed the little stack to Crosson, who peered slowly and somberly at each picture in turn. On a few his gaze lingered, eyes intense and brow wrinkled.

"Can I take these back with me?" he asked finally.

"Sure. I have the negatives," Morgan answered.

"I'll show them to Hall. Blown up they'll reveal a lot." He replaced them in the envelope and slipped them into his shirt pocket.

"Their personal stuff is in a room at the back," explained Brower. "But I guess you can let that go till tomorrow."

"I'll take a quick look," said Crosson. Turning to the Eskimo, he said, "Thanks, Clair."

Brower had obviously tried to store and arrange everything neatly, but it was still a jumble: the rubber raft—cases of chili—mounds of soggy newspapers, magazines, maps, books, and separate papers—broken fishing rods—crushed baskets—battered suitcases—a pile of rubber boots—extra sleeping bags.

Crosson reached down and picked up a water-stained book. "I gave Will this," he murmured, almost talking to himself. "*Arctic Village*. Looks like he was reading it on the plane . . . tucked his reading glasses in and put on a rubber band."

He put the book down and stood staring at the pathetic assortment. "There's that old typewriter of his over there. Still has a sheet of paper in it." He crossed the room and crouched down before the black Royal portable. Many of its keys were twisted out of position, the ribbon torn and the two reels warped. But the sturdy iron frame was intact, though battered. Leaning down close, Crosson read the two long paragraphs typed on the paper. "This part's about my dog, Mickey," he said, reading on, "the time he was chased by a bear." Finished reading, he straightened up. "I told him that story when he was staying . . ."

He turned to Brower. "Charlie, I'm tired. Really tired. I need to get rested up for the flight back. You have a bed somewhere that I—"

"All ready for you," offered Brower, "Bob too, if he wants. Sleep as long as you like. When you get up we'll give you a good breakfast and you'll be ready for Walakpa. I'll go there with you, if you think it'll help."

"Thanks. But I don't think I'll bother with that. The pictures and talking to Clair and Stan and Frank, that'll be enough. Forget about going out to Walakpa. I'd rather use the time getting back to Fairbanks, beat any bad weather that may come up."

"Oh. I just thought—"

"Till I saw those pictures I wasn't sure," Crosson said. "You can tell from the photos that it'd be a waste of time going out there. The engine's all smashed and jammed back into the cockpit, almost back into the cabin. The valves and switches, the instrument board, everything's gone. When a little plane like that goes down, there isn't much left. A sheared-off wing, a few broken windows, a crumpled elevator, an upside-down cabin, they don't tell much. I'd rather use the time getting home."

"Yeah, OK, whatever you say," Brower relented. "How about this. While you're sleeping we'll put the bodies aboard. Don't need you for that. You and Bob rest up, and when you're ready everything'll be waiting for you."

"Thanks. The space for them in the plane is marked off, where the seats are taken out." Ten minutes later in an upstairs room at the Brower house Crosson lay fast asleep. Gleason preferred to stay with the plane near his wireless, stretching out in a sleeping bag.

On sleds the two bodies were pulled through the village to the lagoon. An Associated Press story pictured the scene: "A forlorn little group of mourners, the dozen white settlers and a large gathering of Eskimos, stood silently by at Barrow for a last farewell to the strangers killed on a trip to see them. They shuffled about and talked in whispers as the bodies were laid carefully in the grieving Crosson's airplane."

The storied Joe Crosson, old friend of Wiley Post, called "Alaska's ace pilot," or "the mercy pilot," for his many exciting rescue missions.

The Fairchild in which he flew to Barrow in bad weather to bring back the two bodies to Fairbanks. Here it has skis. Crosson used pontoons.

Charles Brower's house in Barrow, in wintertime.

Brower's place in its more inviting summer aspect. It was in one of the sheds at the right that the bodies of Rogers and Post were kept awaiting their return home.

Plane Bearing Bodies Of Victims Detained At Fairbanks By Storms

Pilot Crosson, Friend Of Post And Rogers, Hopes To Take Off For Seattle Today

CROWD FLOCKS TO RIVER TO PAY HOMAGE TO FAMED DEAD

Embalming Completed — Rex Beach Recalls Chat With Pair At Juneau—Part Played By Wives Revealed

By Bernard N. Stone
(Reporter, Fairbanks News-Miner)

Copyright, 1935, By The Associated Press

Fairbanks, Alaska, Aug. 17—(AP)—Weeping skies and lowering murk impeded the flight of Joe Crosson out of Alaska with the bodies of Will Rogers and Wiley Post today.

Ace pilot of the Far North, Crosson brought the bodies of the cowboy philosopher and 'round-the-world flier here

THE ATLANTA CONSTITUTION

The Sunday Constitution Leads in Home Delivered, City and Trading Territory Circulation!

The South's Standard Newspaper

VOL. LXVIII., No. 67.

ONLY MORNING NEWSPAPER PUBLISHED IN ATLANTA

ATLANTA, GA., SUNDAY MORNING, AUGUST 18, 1935.

Entered at Atlanta Postoffice As Second-Class Mail Matter.

A. P. Service
United Press
N. A. N. A.

FAMED PILOT BATTLES THROUGH RAGING RAINS TO FLY
BODIES OF WILL ROGERS, WILEY POST TO FAIRBANKS

100 Reported Slain In French Colony By Ethiopian Tribe

Il Duce and Selassie May Direct Battles

LONDON, Aug. 17.—(AP)—A possibility of Benito Mussolini, dictator of Italy, and Emperor Haile Selassie I, ruler of Abyssinia, personally directing their troops into action was seen this weekend...

MUSSOLINI SPURNS POWERS' PROPOSAL

Sweeping Concessions to Duce, Financial Support Are Offered To Avert Impending Warfare.

ROME, Aug. 17...

Rome Demands Support in Overpowering African Kingdom on Basis of Incident; Claims Largest Standing Army.

ROAD FUND DETAIL SENT BY WALLACE TO HIGHWAY BOARD

Washington Authorities Hope Letter Will Clear Way for Releasing Millions for State Projects.

WASHINGTON, Aug. 17.—(AP)—Secretary Wallace sent the Georgia Highway Board a letter today setting forth conditions which the administration hoped will open the way to release of Georgia's impounded federal road millions...

Talmadge Favors '$3 Auto Tags' As Presidential Campaign Plank

Outstanding Advocate of State's Rights Veers From Accustomed Course To Urge National Price-Fixing; Laughs Off N. Y. 'Racket' Charges.

Eugene Talmadge, an outstanding advocate of the rights of the states, veered from his path yesterday by charging that the fixing of prices of automobile tags should be an issue in the national campaign of 1936.

Naturally, Talmadge would have the universal price of the tags fixed at $3...

Depends on Board.

Whether the long-drawn controversy...

Laughs Off Charges.

The governor laughed off the charges, pointing out that any out-of-state citizen who buys a tag must...

LEADERS ABANDON UTILITY BILL HOPE, SPEED TAX ACTION

Sunday Conference Planned To Reach Agreement on $250,000,000 Bill; Swift Finish Seen.

WASHINGTON, Aug. 17.—(AP)—Congressional leaders tonight gauged the remaining administration program and found it no takeshipre that presages an adjournment expected in mid-September...

Georgia Licenses Stopped.

The New York official had ordered Commissioner Lewis J. Valentine, of the New York city police and other police officials to stop all cars bearing Georgia licenses.

Moseley said he "understood" that...

The Chairman Deputy "flatly" denied. He exhibited an application blank...

Return to States Is Planned Today If Weather Permits

Funeral for Rogers To Be in Los Angeles

NEW YORK, Aug. 17.—(AP)—Funeral services for Will Rogers were tentatively set tonight for late Thursday at 2 p. m. in Los Angeles.

The widow announced through Jesse Jones, chairman of the Reconstruction Finance Corporation, a family friend...

LINDBERGH ASSISTS BEREAVED FAMILY

Linen - Wrapped Bodies Are Taken to Undertaking Establishment for Preparation for Burial.

FAIRBANKS, Alaska, Aug. 17.—(AP)—Weeping skies and lowered mist impeded the attempt today to start the bodies of the two Alaskans with the bodies of Will Rogers and Wiley Post toward...

Sorrowing Alaskans Bow in Silent Homage as Two World Figures in Death, Are Brought to End of First Homeward Flight.

The two bodies arrive in Los Angeles from Seattle. Crosson was aboard as a passenger.

The Rogers family en route home to Los Angeles from Maine. (left to right) Theda Blake, sister of Mrs. Rogers, son Jim, daughter Mary, Mrs. Rogers, son Will, Jr.

The flight home began early next morning, plagued by bad weather, and at one point was caught in a torrential thunderstorm, full of huge jagged lightning bolts. Almost every mile of the journey was closely followed by newspaper readers across the country. Perhaps the *Atlanta Constitution*'s eight-column banner headline went a little beyond most others, yet telling only the plain truth: *Famed Pilot Battles Through Raging Rains to Fly Bodies of Will Rogers, Wiley Post to Fairbanks.*

The *New York Times* focused on the arrival in Fairbanks and the landing on the Chena River where a crowd waited, Lillian among them:

> Fairbanks, Alaska, Aug. 17: Through the same murky Arctic skies which lured them to death, the bodies of Will Rogers and Wiley Post were borne to Fairbanks today in the first phase of the long journey home.
>
> Joe Crosson, ace pilot of the Far North and close friend of the two men, made the dangerous 500-mile flight from Point Barrow in four-and-one-half hours.
>
> Crosson's pontooned plane alighted on the surface of the Chena River here at 7:35 A.M.... All Fairbanks flocked to the river bank . . . between lines of sorrowing Alaskans the linen-wrapped bodies were moved to an undertaking establishment.
>
> Crosson and his flight companion, Robert Gleason, radio operator, were near exhaustion from the perilous 1000-mile round trip flight to the fringe of northern civilization. Nevertheless, Crosson said he would proceed on the homeward journey as soon as possible . . .

At Fairbanks there was a stopover of one day. Then the bodies, now embalmed, were transferred to a larger, more modern airplane, the company's Lockheed Electra. The thousand-mile journey to Seattle included two stops, at Whitehorse in Canada for refueling, and Vancouver. Again Crosson was at the controls, this time with a co-pilot in addition to a radio operator. On toward Seattle he flew, picking up as escort a full squadron of Navy fighters, sent from Seattle to meet them.

At the Seattle airport a huge mob waited to greet "the funeral plane," as the ship was now being called by the papers. That same day the bodies were surrendered to other authorities acting for the families and prepared for the long journey home, Post to Oklahoma, Rogers to Los Angeles.

Joe Crosson's mournful odyssey had ended. The painful memory of it would never leave him.

12

WHEN THEY ASKED HER where she wanted to have Will buried, in Oklahoma or in Los Angeles, Betty said she didn't know, she was simply too drained and exhausted to think straight.

The funeral, then, where should the funeral be?

In Los Angeles, she said after a while, because she just couldn't move another inch from home, couldn't get on another plane or train, couldn't face or walk through another mob of sad-eyed people.

The funeral service was held at Forest Lawn in Glendale on the afternoon of August 22—earlier that morning the casket reposed under a tree outside, and about fifty thousand people, or a hundred thousand, or whatever the true number was, filed past it. The services were held in a little chapel called the Wee Kirk o' the Heather, which had special pews for not much more than a hundred people, all of them admitted by special invitation.

Among those in the chapel was one of Will's closest friends, writer and fellow actor Irvin Cobb (he was in Will's last picture, *Steamboat Round the Bend*). As soon as Cobb came out of the chapel after the ceremony he wrote a little piece about it for the papers. Of course, newspapers everywhere told the main story of that day in great detail: how nationwide radio went silent for an hour; how the Hollywood studios closed and movie screens everywhere went black; how people in small towns stood with heads bowed for two minutes; how a thousand cities big and small held memorial services, including New York, Chicago, and Boston. Cobb's little piece appeared in a number of papers, but it tended to get lost among the flashier news of the big event. Here's some of what he wrote:

> . . . Through miles of sun-drenched streets, to the music of the sputtering motorcycles of a uniformed cop escort, some of us rode with Will's widow and his children and his people the twenty miles from his ranch in Santa Monica canyon to a tiny chapel that was like a chalice cut out of some luminous stone, cunningly set in a toy mountain above the city whose millions at that point stood silent to join in spirit with the thing we were about to do.
>
> The burying ground gates behind us had fences formed of silent humanity, and the parched hills beyond us were black with thousands. As we went up the small slope to the opened doors I saw one flower piece that was a flying machine, one that was an enormous Old Glory, and others in other shapes, and I saw a shabby little lonesome boy—how he got through the police lines I'll never know—laying on the lawn along with those great masterpieces of the florist's craft, with a sweaty fistful of marigolds that couldn't have cost more than two bits . . .
>
> Inside the church there were only 125 of us and outside on the grass, hearkening through the loudspeakers, only about 500 more, but already about 75,000 counted individuals had passed the bier where it rested under the shade of a friendly tree, and an estimated number of 150,000 had stood outside the cemetery walls for hours, and twenty-odd thousands were at that moment attending the memorial services over at the Hollywood Bowl, and a great city had ceased from all its activities.
>
> By the dispatches we knew that millions of flags were at half-mast over the nation, and millions of hearts must be at half-mast, too.
>
> I claim the little group in the church was typical of the vast uncounted groups of their fellow mourners throughout the land. I saw an admiral there and a full general of the army, his breast gay with ribbons and I saw also grizzled old cowhands from off the vanished ranges, and humble studio workers . . . I saw a little handful of the

real original American gentlemen, Cherokees from Oklahoma, blood kinsmen of Will, who was so proud of the Indian strain in him. They say the red Indian never cries his grief in public, but these men cried aloud when John Boles tore our hearts out as he sang, "Old Faithful." . . . The preacher, Rev. J. Whitcomb Brougher, was all the better in that he choked up so often in speaking of his friend . . .

It was a short service and a very simple one, just what Will would have liked . . . there were not many figures swathed in mourning— why some of the women had on white summer frocks, with touches of color in them, and that was fine, too, and fitting, because Will loved color and plenty of it . . .

Coming away I said this to myself, and I want to say it again . . . If the preachers are right about it, then on some great day in the morning, with the glory of the everlasting sun shining full on his homely face and on that twisted, shy grin, and on those squinted, whimsical eyes—well, Will, we'll be seeing you!

The choked-up tears of the Rev. Brougher, longtime friend of the Rogers family, were real. He was in the pulpit at Betty's request, and his heartfelt eulogy came from personal knowledge. "There are many echoes," he declared simply, "but only now and then an original voice . . . many people but only now and then an outstanding individual. When a great personality suddenly appears, the world stops in its busy rush to look and listen. . . . Such has been the unique and commanding position of Will Rogers during the last quarter of a century. He has been the one figure in the life of our nation who had drawn to himself the admiration and the love of all classes of people. . . ."

At the close of the service the Rogers family stayed seated while the little church emptied. Then Betty, with Mary and the two sons, went up to the bronze casket where it lay at the foot of the altar. Attendants had been instructed that when the family was alone in the church Mrs. Rogers might ask to have the casket opened. Now they stood waiting for the signal.

Just outside the church a mob of reporters lingered near the loudspeaker that brought the service to those unable to get in. One account caught the last, sad touch of the morning's ritual: "For some minutes there had been silence

WILL ROGERS AND WILEY POST ARE LAID TO REST

NATION AND THRONGS PAY FINAL TRIBUTE

100,000 Persons Mass In Forest Lawn Park At Glendale, Cal.

SERVICES HELD IN DOZENS OF PLACES

Oklahoma City Is Likewise a Scene of Sorrowing Throngs

GLENDALE, Calif., Aug. 22—(AP)—The nation took sad leave today of Will Rogers, who "never saw a man I didn't like."

While the world-famed humorist, actor and philosopher was eulogized in scores of solemn memorials, 100,000 persons massed at Forest Lawn Memorial Park.

Starting at sunrise—and before—the crowds came for the bare privilege of filing past his body, as it lay in state in a tiny enclosure of pine and olive trees. An estimated 50,000 passed the bier before noon.

Then, after brief, simple services for the family and closest friends, the body was laid to rest awhile in a vault at Forest Lawn. There it will await ultimate removal to Rogers' native Oklahoma.

At almost the same time in Oklahoma City, other sorrowing throngs bade farewell to Wiley Post, ace

Last Tributes

Please Turn to Page 2

Entire Nation Honors Rogers And Post Today

Memorial Services To Be Held at Same Time as Funerals of Crash Victims

46 Planes to Rise Here

Home Town of Flyer Pays Tribute in Short Rites

By The Associated Press

Airplane motors will roar, prayers will be whispered, bells tolled and funeral services are held in the afternoon for the actor-humorist at Los Angeles and for the globe-girdling flyer at Oklahoma City, legions of friends will memorialize them elsewhere.

President Roosevelt will be represented at the two principal services by Army and Navy officers. They will present wreaths in his behalf.

The Motion Picture Producers and Distributors of America announce that more than 12,000 theaters in all sections of the nation will be darkened for two minutes during the funeral hour as a tribute to Rogers.

All Film Studios to Close

All film studios, including the one at which Rogers was a star, will be closed during the services. It will be the first time in history studios have closed so long for an individual.

On this side of the nation, forty-six planes, fl——
ers, will roar
ute to Post.
Floyd Benne
neral service
homa City.
five planes,
Foreign Wars
In Iowa, c
Moines ceme
College at A
cheering crov
In Des Moi:
two minutes
trayal of the
ture "State F
In many c
Calif., flags
until after tl
fices at the
Phoenix wil
Frank Merri
day called t
state to obse
begining at
standard tin
light time).

200,000 Pay Last Tribute At Funeral For Rogers

Demonstration of Love for Cowboy Sage Without Comparison

All Walks of Life Join in Rites to Humorist

By CAROLYN ANSPACHER
Chronicle Staff Writer

HOLLYWOOD, Aug. 22—Will Rogers came home today as he promised—returning to the people he loved for a few brief hours, before leaving them forever.

As the Nation paused to do him honor, more than 200,000 persons of this Southern California community united in a mammoth demonstration fashioned of love and respect such

---

100,000 Mass at Cemetery To Pass Before Will's Bier

All Walks of Life Assembled in Most Amazing Spectacle of Generation

GLENDALE, Aug. 22 (AP)—A gentle, homely man, with a cowlick of hair, and a side-winding smile, today stirred into existence the most amazing human spectacle of a generation.

across the grass—faces, lined and seamed with age, blooming with youth, touched with a new grief.

The file came on. Consciously or not, they must have felt the truth of the words:

Rogers' burial was at Forest Lawn Cemetery in Glendale, Los Angeles. A throng of a quarter million filed by the closed coffin in the five hours before the afternoon service. Some years later the body was transferred to Rogers' hometown, Claremore, Oklahoma.

San Francisco Chronicle

THE CITY'S ONLY HOME~OWNED NEWSPAPER

RATURES

High Low
ork .. 84 72
, ... 70 64
City.. 82 68
leans . 94 78

CXLVII. NO. 39   CCC   SAN FRANCISCO, CAL., FRIDAY, AUGUST 23, 1935   DA

TEARS BLOT THE JESTER'S QUIPS

The day of Rogers' funeral in Glendale, the Hollywood Bowl was filled for a memorial service. Prayers and eulogies along with hymns and Rogers' favorite songs sung by famous artists left not a dry eye in the stadium. Across the nation movie screens went dark, the Hollywood studios shut down, and the whole Los Angeles area came to a standstill.

WILEY POST RESTS IN NATIVE EARTH

Oklahoma Thousands Mourn Death of Famous Aviator.

OKLAHOMA CITY, Aug. 22.—(AP)—The body of Wiley Post rested in a crypt in Fairlawn Mausoleum tonight after funeral services as simple as the rustic surroundings he left to fly to undying fame.

The brief church rites ended a day of tribute to the stocky flyer, who with Will Rogers, another famous son of Oklahoma, crashed to death on a flying vacation near Point Barrow, Alaska.

Earlier, airplanes droned a requiem high overhead and then swooped low to scatter flowers over his coffin, the governor of the state delivered a eulogy and more than 15,000 persons crowded the corridors of the Capitol to pay a final tribute. A section of the heavy marble railing about the rotunda collapsed, but no one was injured.

Friends Carry Body.

As soon as the church services were finished, the building was cleared of everyone but members of the immediate family. For a few brief moments they were alone with their dead.

Then they signaled to national guardsmen and city officers and a path was cleared from the door to a waiting hearse.

Borne by men who had been close friends of the famous pilot, the body was placed in the hearse and taken along crowded streets to the mausoleum.

The First Baptist Church was filled to overflowing with hundreds more gathered outside. Post's widow and mother made their way with difon the loudspeaker. Then the reporters became aware of sobs. They glanced at the horn. The sobs grew louder. Inside, Mrs. Rogers had stopped for a last look at the coffin. Beside her was the microphone. There was a moment or two of anguish. Then someone switched off the loudspeaker."

The body was placed in a temporary vault at Forest Lawn, awaiting Betty's decision as to permanent burial. Will's estate was probated at nearly three million dollars, so she continued to live at the ranch in Santa Monica. Not until nine years had passed did she decide to have the body returned to Oklahoma for interment in Will's old hometown of Claremore. It was as if she knew that the time had come to join him.

A month after the transfer, Betty herself died, a cancer victim. She lies beside her husband in Claremore.

13

IT WAS THE PLANE'S FAULT, declared the U.S. Bureau of Air Commerce in announcing the result of its accident investigation, two weeks after the funeral. Whoever might be responsible for the plane's condition they didn't say.

Because the structural changes had altered the plane's original aerodynamic design (new wings, new engine, pontoons, extra gas tanks), the only license that could by law be granted was a "restricted" one. This forbade the carrying of passengers, allowing only the pilot and legitimate "crew," and permitting only a limited range of use. In Post's relaxed view, this didn't bar Will Rogers because he could be seen as helping in small ways to man and care for the plane and its "cargo."

The fact that the various changes had resulted in a decided "nose-heavy" condition was not at first known to the bureau's licensing arm. In any case, everyone agreed that Post, who was one of the most knowledgeable among aviators with a voluminous understanding of plane performance, would know best about that. Whether the plane should have been personally flown by a bureau inspector, tested aloft for "airworthiness" before getting a license—rather than just looking it over and checking the written records of the work done—became a question never settled. Even after study of the regulations, the licensing of the plane was largely explained by the fact that these were early days—still open-cockpit, white-scarf days—in the policing of the aviation industry (and barely thirty years since the Wrights first flew).

Post himself, in one of his curiously unguarded moments, stated that structural changes to the little red plane caused an imbalance that needed constant correction by the pilot. To reporters in Seattle, the day after the pontoons were applied, he had this to say, certainly half joking: "I don't know much about Alaska. I haven't had much experience flying planes with pontoons. I wonder how it's going to work out." Later he confided in his friend Joe Crosson, and a few others, the undoubted fact that the plane was a cranky handler because its center of gravity had shifted some back toward the tail, dropping the nose. Rogers himself talked—though without understanding the implications of what he said in joking fashion—about having to position himself toward the cabin's rear as "ballast."

Some degree of imbalance in a plane, of instability fore and aft, is acceptable as a trade-off, the price to be paid for blending or adjusting a variety of factors, such as fuel consumption, speed, and distribution of storage. Post himself, in the 1931 book he wrote (see Bibliography) about his first world-girdling flight, discusses the problem (referring to alterations made on his first plane, the famous *Winnie Mae*). What he says applies handily to the little red plane as well:

> . . . then came the problem of loading . . . so many things can happen to planes that are badly loaded. A tail-heavy plane, flying through the air with its elevator and stabilizer at maximum nose-down position, more or less has the tendency to "mush" along with undue lifting force exerted on the wing and tail surfaces. This increases the resistance offered by the air, and slows the ship down, increasing correspondingly its fuel consumption. The reverse situation, a nose-heavy plane, while better than tail-heaviness, still wears

the pilot out, and sets up undue strains on the top side of the tail assembly. . . .

For his flight around the world he "wanted more fuel, and I had a navigator and a more constant weight to carry. If I put the constant weight directly on the center of gravity where it would make the least difference, I would be all right." But his navigator couldn't fit in the small space available, "and if I put him ahead of the c.g. I would have to carry the fuel behind, and as soon as the gasoline load grew light the ship would need a lot of trimming to keep it from growing nose-heavy. Landing with an empty tail, a tired pilot, and a 75-mile speed," was not an inviting prospect.

Substitute Rogers for Harold Gatty, who accompanied Post on his first world flight, and the problem is the same. The imponderable factor is the second change, the change in landing gear, the way the pontoons increased the little red plane's front-end heaviness by adding drag.

What Post does not discuss in his book, or anywhere else, is the catastrophic effect of a sudden power loss in an unbalanced ship. So long as the engine is running, a competent pilot can readily "trim" the craft, make the needed adjustments at the controls, and fly the plane any distance, taking off and landing without fear of mishap. As soon as power is lost, however, a nose-heavy plane will dip at the front, slowly or sharply, and go into a nosedive. If it is high enough off the ground it may have time to straighten out for a gliding touchdown. But if the engine quits when the plane is still low to the ground— below three hundred feet, say—recovery from a precipitous nosedive will be extremely difficult.

That's what happened to Post, decided the Air Commerce Bureau. His engine stalled on him before he'd gotten high enough, and he had no time to pull the nose up for a landing. What made it stall was a matter for conjecture. It might have been due "to the engine having become cool while standing on the lagoon, or to ice or water condensate forming in the carburetor." Another bureau document put it differently: "With the moisture in the air as it existed that day, and the temperature as it was reported, ice could have developed in the carburetor. Either that, or the spray from the water in taking off could have entered the scoops and in that way caused icing," which cut off the flow of gas.

That the engine may simply have run out of gas because one of the six tanks emptied before Post realized it and switched to a full tank, wasn't considered in the official report. But the possibility did occur to many observers, then and since, the theory of course remaining beyond proof. (It could not have been that all six tanks went dry, because 270 gallons would not have been consumed in five and a half hours in the air.)

Inevitably with issuance of the government report, Post's reputation as an aviator suffered. He was flying a type of craft "with which he was wholly unfamiliar," pointed out the *New York Herald-Tribune*:

> . . . it was a hybrid machine pieced together under Post's direction from the parts of several airplanes. . . . No pilot in New York who knew the globe-girdling flyer intimately could recall that he had ever flown a marine-type plane, other than on a casual local trip. . . . The ship was transferred from wheels to pontoons at Seattle, and veteran seaplane pilots said that the unaccustomed bulk of these floats might be disastrous even to a pilot of Post's ability if he found himself in a jam.

The unspoken charge was that Post had acted hastily and on impulse, that the pontoons were an ill-considered afterthought and had not been properly figured into the stability equation. With all his experience and skill as a flyer, he'd been caught by the one "jam" neither he nor any other pilot could handle, a sudden power loss in a nose-heavy plane at a low altitude.

The hybrid plane and the pontoons were Post's personal responsibility. Whether the stalled engine could also be laid against him, nobody would attempt to say.

Few came forward to defend Post. One who did was his old pal, the loyal Joe Crosson. Almost indignantly he issued a statement declaring that Post was in no way to blame for what happened, that "he was a careful flyer, not an air desperado, and all the stories to the contrary are not true." Over and over Post had shown "his great skill as a pilot. He was one of the best. I can't say what caused the crash, and I don't believe anybody ever will. . . . But I know this—whatever went wrong was not due to poor flying on the part of Wiley Post."

Two whaleboats carrying a dozen hooded and parka-wrapped Eskimos glided into Walakpa Lagoon. Behind them came the Brower launch, again with Dave Brower in charge. Slowly the three boats edged up to the plane wreck. Under Dave's direction the Eskimos, wielding a variety of tools, pulleys, and ropes, began dismantling the smashed ship.

It was now September 6, three weeks after the crash. At first, the Air Commerce Bureau had ordered the wreck to be left undisturbed, pending inspection by a bureau officer (no "accident report" specialists existed then). After Crosson reported on the accident, it was decided that sending an agent to the scene of the crash wasn't required, that such an effort "would not have developed any new information," and that the wreckage could be disposed of. The hard task of taking it apart occupied two whole days. On the evening of September 9 Charlie Brower sat down at his desk and made an entry in his diary. It is worth putting on the record:

> . . . sent 25 men two lighters and our launch to bring the wreck to Barrow. David in charge. They found the wreck as they had left it . . . except that the fuselage has started to fall to pieces where it had been so badly smashed. Took the lighters in the lagoon and lifted the plane piece by piece aboard them . . . while the engine was fished from the bottom of the lagoon where it was buried in two feet of sand with three feet of water to work in . . . after raising the large parts the bottom of the lagoon was combed and every little piece that could be found was saved.
>
> It took the two lighters to raise the engine from the sand and mud underwater but it was finally salvaged with all three props [three blades] attached, one of which was badly bent and hooked under the sand.
>
> The boys returned to Barrow the evening of the 8th and everything was taken in charge by myself, the engine and all accessories

ROGERS-POST CRASH BLAMED ON PLANE

E. L. Vidal's Official Report Says Pontoons Made Craft Nose-Heavy in Take-Offs.

CARBURETOR ICE IS HINTED

Document Absolves World Flier and Explains Reports on Ignored Weather Data.

Special to THE NEW YORK TIMES.

WASHINGTON, Sept. 3.—Nose-heaviness and the possibility that ice had developed in the carburetor of their plane were assigned officially today as the reasons for the fatal crash that took Will Rogers and Wiley Post to their deaths on Aug. 16 in a shallow lagoon near Point Barrow, Alaska.

A report on the accident by Eugene L. Vidal, of Air Commerce, to Secretary Roper resolved all doubts as to its cause in favor of the world-girdling aviator, exonerating him completely from any blame.

The pilot had taken every precaution against placing the life of his passenger in jeopardy, the report held.

The plane's tendency to nose downward on landings and take-offs did not develop until after floats had been substituted for its wheels, the report said. Mr. Post told Pilot Crosson of Pan American Airways at Fairbanks, that he had instructed Mr. Rogers to sit as far to the rear as possible on take-offs and to keep the luggage and equipment well aft, it said.

Friends Wish Post Had Stuck To Winnie Mae

Ship in Which He Crashed Had Pontoons; He Wasn't Well Versed in Seaplanes

Alaska Machine a Hybrid

Flyer Himself Assembled It From Various Planes

Although the flying feats that brought Wiley Post world-wide fame all were achieved in a Lockheed plane, the Winnie Mae, and he was killed in a ship of the same make, he was flying a type of craft with which he was almost wholly unfamiliar when he and Will Rogers crashed in Alaska. It was a hybrid craft, put together under Post's supervision out of several different flying machines attached far less familiar than to the fast plane equipped rather than the plane Post was accustomed.

No pilot in North globe-girdling type plane, others recall that he ever local trip, until transferred flight to Seattle and said that the these floats might to a pilot of Post himself in a surf.

Wouldn't It H.

Those inclined as Post himself wondering whet might not have had stuck to Winnie Mae, w before he started and ordered put action of the Representatives Smithsonian H called the seen ence of the Win following records Post had estab-

Post's Plane 'Nose-Heavy,' Says Crosson

Aviator Reports Badly-Balanced Ship Due to Installing New Pontoons

WASHINGTON, Sept. 3.—A suggestion that a plane made nose-heavy by pontoon equipment sent Wiley Post and Will Rogers to their deaths in Alaska was contained today in a Commerce Department report on the accident.

Eugene Vidal, air commerce chief and writer of the memorandum issued by the department, said Joe Crosson, the pilot who brought the bodies back to the United States, told him of this trouble.

Told Rogers to Sit Well Back

"Mr. Post substituted for his wheel landing gear a pair of pontoons at ... w will ... n that ... st in- ... n Air- ... become ... s, and ... ndings ... ructed ... far as ... equip- ... ke-off ... d. ... believe ... ine to ... climb, ... would ... Barrow ... ly af- ... ering. ... he fog ... search ... e in a ... flying ... take- ... e and ... could ... on as ... e, the

Pilot Crosson Warned Post Of Bad Weather Conditions

POINT BARROW, Alaska, Aug. 16 (AP)—Pilot Joe Crosson left here tonight to transport the bodies of Will Rogers and Wiley Post by plane to Fairbanks en route to the United States.

When Post and Rogers first discussed hopping off for Point Barrow yesterday no weather reports were available for that Arctic region. Crosson counseled them against making the flight.

Later, a report was received that there was a dense fog along the route and the thermometer registered 45 degrees.

Friends quoted Post as saying, "I think we might as well go anyway." Rogers, they said, agreed, declaring "there's lots of lakes we can land on."

As Post prepared the plane for the takeoff, Rogers told those near the ship he was looking forward to seeing Charles Brower, "King of the Arctic," who resides at Point Barrow.

Joe Crosson
Will Return Bodies

Post-Rogers Flight Log

motor being buried in the mud underneath some two feet of water."

placed in a warehouse, the plane with all the pieces was placed alongside my store and is still there. . . . Certainly it is in bad shape wings torn off both pontoons stove in the front end and crumpled up the fuselage broken in a thousand pieces all metal work bent and twisted . . . two pieces of the fuselage are still of some size one still attached to the tail. . . .

Brower knew engines, and one item he noticed credited Post with some presence of mind as the plane dove down out of control: "In looking at the instrument board I found that the switch had been turned off. Evidently the last thing Post had done was to turn it off hoping to save fire as no doubt they did and as there was no stripped gear anywhere the engine must surely have been stopped before the crash."

Of course, the engine had stalled, stopped, before the fatal dive began. Whether an open switch on a dead engine could have caused fire is problematic, as is the idea that, in those last seconds, as he tried desperately to level the plane Post would have thought of or bothered about the switch. But the observation is made by the man who inspected both engine and instrument board as they came from the lagoon, and so deserves recording.

Eventually the engine was returned to its owner, Pratt & Whitney (Post had only rented it), and the propeller to its manufacturer. The instrument panel had originally been part of the *Winnie Mae*, so it was sent back to Mrs. Post, who was the wrecked plane's legal owner. The rest of the wreckage, on orders of Mrs. Post, was loaded aboard the two whaleboats, taken a couple of miles offshore, and sunk in the restless depths of the Arctic Ocean.

14

NO, SHE TOLD HERSELF FIRMLY. She wouldn't give up. She'd do it. Her father would *want* her to do it.

Sometime in the two or three weeks following the funeral, her young spirit still badly bruised, Mary Rogers made up her mind about continuing with her acting career. Even while feeling wary as to how she'd react when again on a stage facing an audience, she decided to honor her commitment for Broadway in the fall. Early in September when word came from New York that the new play—a "melodramatic farce" titled *Crime Marches On*—would open at the Morosco Theatre on October 23, she replied that she was on her way. Reaching New York on September 9, she plunged headlong into rehearsals.

Whatever secret resource it was that enabled her to go on, even while distrusting her ability to do it, some part of her inspiration must have come from the memory of her father's early encouragement of her ambitions. Fitting, in that case, was the fact that on the same day she arrived in New York, her father's last film, *Steamboat Round the Bend*, had its gala opening at Radio City Music Hall. It was as if he'd come east with her, and now was there in New York, at a theater within walking distance of the Morosco, watching over her.

Crime Marches On opened as announced on October 23 with an unusually large cast, some forty characters, and Mary as the romantic lead, opposite Elisha Cook, Jr. and Charles Halton. The reviews, disappointingly, were mixed, all the way from very good to very bad. Mary herself won satisfying praise from the critics, influenced a little by who she was, no doubt. Brooks Atkinson of the *New York Times* found the play to be badly staged and decidedly unfunny, "an ear-splitting fandango in the booby hatch . . . a drama that shouts itself out of existence before the evening is over." Mary he spotlights as "the daughter of the lamented Will, and a beautiful young woman in her own very winning right. She remains cool and lovely in the vortex of a shrill version of Donnybrook Fair."

More favorable was the view of Robert Garland in the *World-Telegram*: "Mad, merry, melodramatic, and malicious . . . had the audience in a dither . . . the season's most amazing prank . . . hardboiled and hilarious, and good, red blood-and-thunder." His praise of Mary was freely expressed if a bit awkwardly: "Mary Rogers, daughter of the late, beloved Will, is a credit to her family as Phyllis . . . pleasing to the most exacting playgoers' senses, she is an ever-present boon to the exhibit at the Morosco." (The curiously convoluted language reflects only the critic's difficulty in finding new ways to say the same thing week after week.)

Crime managed to hold on for little more than a month, and by November 30 it was gone. With that, Mary found herself mentioned in the drama columns as being sought for a number of good roles. In the end, however, she chose to avoid the strains of another pressure cooker Broadway production by going off Broadway. Her month of performances in *Crime* had proved more of an ordeal than she'd expected, showing itself as an unaccountable nervousness and fidgeting while on stage. After the curtain went up, seldom had she been able to relax in her character or feel really comfortable looking out over the footlights. She thought the deliberately frantic noise level of the farce-drama would help distract her, but the opposite had happened. Unusual or insistent noise acted not as a distraction, but as a reminder, recalling the raucous glaring of the loudspeaker in *Ceiling Zero*.

On January 13, 1936, she opened in a theater in Newark, New Jersey, in support of the great old-time player William Gillette (creator of the stage Sherlock Holmes many years before, and now a robust eighty). The play, *Three Wise Fools*, was headed for Broadway as a summer replacement, but with that, Mary's brave effort caught up with her, and all at once. On stage during the fourth night of that first week in Newark she grew increasingly nervous and upset, so that she barely made it through the final scene. Trembling as the curtain fell, she left the stage with head splitting and hands unable to hold a cup. A doctor, summoned to her dressing room, didn't need long to reach the discouraging diagnosis: nervous breakdown. Next day, limply despondent and accompanied by a nurse, she was on a train heading home to California.

Still she refused to give up. Though it required several weeks of rest and medical care before she felt fully recovered, by the end of March she was ready to give it another try. This time, she courageously determined, she would set herself the ultimate test, appearing on the same stage she occupied the night her father was killed. Exactly a year to the day after that tragedy—on August 15th—she vowed she would be on stage at Lakewood. She'd get ready for the ordeal, she decided, by saturating herself in the life of the stage, appearing in every performance of every play at Lakewood leading up to that night. Involved would be at least ten plays, for some seventy performances, in the space of two and a half months. She'd make the Lakewood stage so familiar and friendly an environment that no bad memory of the real world could intrude for long.

Her telegram to the Lakewood director, Herbert Swett, announcing her wish to return for the 1936 season, brought an appreciative notice from the *Somerset Reporter*:

> Mary Rogers, easily the most popular young actress who has appeared with the Lakewood players in the last ten years, is coming back to Lakewood for her third summer . . . A telegram states that she will be on hand when rehearsals start . . . welcome news to Lakewood patrons. At first greeted as Will Rogers' daughter, the actress won a devoted following through her own talent, and there was almost a feeling of personal loss last summer when her family tragedy, the death of Will Rogers, forced her to leave the company the week she was playing the feminine lead in "Ceiling Zero."
>
> On Broadway last summer Miss Rogers was the leading woman in "Crime Marches On," and was also in the revival of "Three Wise Fools" with William Gillette. She was forced to leave the cast of the latter play because of a nervous breakdown, from which she has now completely recovered at her California home . . .

Again, it was a valiant decision, no doubt talked over with her mother, but at last flowing from her own naturally buoyant spirit. If an added cause is wanted, it can be reasonably suggested that her father, through her rereading of one of his earlier letters, actually played a crucial part in her decision—a letter she kept all her life and which is now on file at the Will Rogers Memorial Museum in Claremore. That she spent some part of those housebound months of her recovery looking over the little cache of her father's correspondence to her is not unlikely (several letters and postcards going back ten years).

Written to Mary in 1932 on her nineteenth birthday, the letter is a simple but straightforward declaration of love and affectionate faith. It is easy to imagine her in the doleful hours of her recovery reading it with eyes brimming over:

My Dear Daughter.

My! Just think our little girl is nineteen years old today. Sounds old to you. But it's so short a time to Dad and Mama.

You was born on Sunday afternoon in Rogers, Ark. at little "Mamoos" house. Dad was playing a little vaudeville Theater in Houston, Texas, the Majestic. I got the wire and went on the stage for my matinee and told em about you. So you wasn't very old before your old Dad commenced bragging on you, and he hasn't stopped for 19 years, and he never will.

You have been a dandy fine Girl. Sometimes we old ones dont see eye to eye with you kids. But its us that dont stop to see your modern viewpoint. Times change but Human Nature dont. You are your mother in a 1932 setting.

You are going to leave us for the first time. You are going over to Europe. It dont sound far when I go or when Mama and I go. But it does seem far when Dad's little girl goes. We hope you have a fine time, we know you will benefit by the trip.

We are proud of you Honey, and our missing you will be in some part offset by our Happiness at your pleasure. Nineteen years old. You are our daughter now, and no longer our little girl, and your happiness will always be our Happiness.

Old Dad.

What he "told" the audience at the Majestic Theater about his new baby that Sunday in 1913 he doesn't say. It must have been more than just the simple news of the birth. His vaudeville act then was a display of trick and fancy roping, enlivened by humorous patter, funny-wise observations on the day's people and events. He was a name in vaudeville then but was still a couple of years away from his big break, a featured spot with the Ziegfeld Follies. In his comment to the Majestic audience that Sunday there must have been a few jokes about his new baby daughter, a wry laugh or two about the responsibilities of parenthood, maybe, that brought a knowing laugh from his listeners. All of this unwritten part of the story, no doubt long ago told to the delighted Mary, would have come back to her as she reread his letter.

INDEPENDENT-REPORTER (MAINE)

Mary Sets A Record At Lakewood

MARY ROGERS

Mary's first try at Broadway came in a comedy (see below). Critics praised her but the experience led only to a nervous breakdown.

The next year, in a second determined effort, she threw herself into a season of summer stock (right). A movie contract resulted and all hoped she had at last escaped the heavy memory of her father's tragic end.

INDEPENDENT-REPORTER (MAINE)

GEORGE BUSHAR and JOHN TUERK offer

CRIME MARCHES ON

A Melodramatic Farce by
BERTRAND ROBINSON and MAXWELL HAWKINS
Staged by **EDWARD CLARK LILLEY**

with

Elisha Cook, Jr.   Mary Rogers
Charles D. Brown   Charles Halton
Donald Randolph and a Company of 40
Settings by John Root

EVES. $1.10 to $3.30—MATS. WED. & SAT. 55c. to $2.20. SEATS TOMORROW

MOROSCO Theatre, 45th W. of B'way **Opening WED. NIGHT at 8:40**

Nine weeks after Rogers' death, his last movie opened on Broadway at the Hippodrome. It was the same day (October 22) that his daughter, Mary, in a brave effort to resume her acting career, opened in her first Broadway part at the Morosco.

On May 8th Mary left home for Lakewood. Not caring for another transcontinental journey by train, still wary of flying, she went by boat, a leisurely trip from Los Angeles to New York by way of the Panama Canal. Her arrival in Skowhegan was duly noted by the *Somerset Reporter*, which commented that "the charming lass whose future seems particularly bright, having inherited some of those priceless talents of her beloved father, was showered with greetings upon her arrival . . . no sooner had she started unpacking than she went to the theater to get her part in *Mr. Shaddy*, the initial Lakewood vehicle."

How did it feel, she was asked, to be back in Skowhegan for a third season, and unspoken in the background of the question was the all-too-vivid memory of the previous year's tragic ending. Mary's response was perky and bright as she tried to deflect any somber note in her return: "The people here have been so lovely to me that it feels like coming home . . . between performances and rehearsals I hope to get in some tennis, and ride horseback, and hike through the country."

Her first sight of the stage came that evening when she went alone and paused at the rear of the hall to gaze at it, bare and empty, over the rows of seats. Only a slight jab of apprehension coursed through her, but no real distress, a reaction that surprised her. Two weeks later on opening night, May 30, she sailed through her part in "Mr. Shaddy." Her first entrance on stage was hailed by the sympathetic audience with hearty applause—she paused only long enough to throw a smiling look of appreciation across the footlights. At the play's finish the repeated curtain calls were even more enthusiastically cheered.

By the time August 15th arrived, she'd taken demanding roles in all ten Lakewood productions, not missing a performance, and without any serious sign of excessive tension. Even then, however, for the performance on the anniversary of the tragedy, August 15th, her brother Will, Jr., called Bill, flew in to be with her backstage, ready to take charge if anything went wrong. (His presence was noted by the *Reporter*, though not the reason for it, saying that he'd arrived on Thursday, August 13th, and left four days later, on the 17th: "His smile is reminiscent of his father's, and like the rest of the family he was democratic, pleasant to meet, friendly.")

Nothing happened at the performance on the 15th, nothing bad. The play was the lighthearted *Star Light, Star Bright*, by Owen Davis, and so lost in her lines and her character was she that she actually forgot the day's special significance. Only as the curtain rang down to the sound of loud applause and cheering did she suddenly recall what day it was. The pain of the abrupt recollection was intense but it lasted only a moment. When she took her bows with the rest of the cast her smile again flashed warm and bright.

Seven more plays were given at Lakewood after *Star Light*, and Mary, undisturbed by nerves, took leading roles in five of them, appearing in fifteen plays out of the seventeen given that season. It was, the *Reporter* stated, "a record for a feminine performer at Lakewood, and probably in any stock company."

Her season's bold experiment in Skowhegan, and its marked success at showcasing her real talents, had not gone unnoticed on the West Coast. In the audience for at least one night of *Star Light* were executives from two Hollywood studios (Max Gordon and Harry Goetz of Republic Pictures, and someone from 20th Century Fox, Rogers' old studio). Word of Fox's interest had reached Lakewood even before that, and by November it had Mary under contract ($2,500 per week, with options). She was, Fox executives all felt, another star in the making—as it had in so many films, the Rogers name would again glitter magically in lights, a rival to such as Crawford, Colbert, Goddard, and Loy. Her first picture was already chosen and in the works, an epic historical drama about the African slave trade, titled *The Last Slaver*.

Then, swiftly and sadly, it all unraveled. Somehow, her determined, year-long try could not heal or overcome the harm done to her by the incredible coincidence of the fictional and the real crashes. (Did she ever know how very close in time the crashes matched, and that her father died while she was actually on stage pretending to feel horror at the fatal crash of Bogart/Davis? Circumstances say she did.)

Though the full picture of the unhappy ending is veiled, it can just be followed by a close look at the few remaining documents.

By mid-December, casting and set design on *The Last Slaver* were finished, and the picture went into rehearsal with a shooting script. Though new to movie-making, for a couple of weeks Mary, now back in Los Angeles and going every day to Fox's Hollywood lot, seemed to take it all in stride. Then suddenly—twice in the course of a month—she pulled out of the picture, vaguely pleading illness. Soon after that she asked to be released from her contract, explaining that she was done with acting. What prompted the decision was never revealed, nor can any clear record of the reasons be found today.

Her initial withdrawal came without warning in early January, when Fox was informed by a family spokesman that Mary "is ill and will be unable to go on with the picture." She was persuaded, apparently, to return, but it didn't last. Early in February she again pulled out, again, as the same family spokesman wrote, "because of illness," its nature still unspecified. At last, in April, she informed Fox that she was quitting for good, then with her Aunt Theda boarded a ship for Europe and stayed away for two months. That the "illness" was not physical is certain, nor is the true reason for the collapse hard to guess. The awful trauma suffered over her father's suddenly dying while she was part of a similar but fictional tragedy, offered as entertainment, at last had corroded her young spirit. The initial shock of the startling coincidence at first had somehow been tempered just enough to make possible all those moments of forgetfulness on the Lakewood and Broadway stages. Perhaps there was something about a movie set—her father's own special world—that made it more intimidating than a stage, perhaps something in the technique of filmmaking itself. Whatever it was, a deep revulsion, a shattering disgust with the whole world of make-believe, seized her. For Mary now her loved father's terrible death was tied luridly to fictional drama, to entertainment. No longer could she face an audience, actual or through a camera, without feeling that same drenching pain she'd felt that morning after the fourth performance of *Ceiling Zero* when she was told about her father. For an audience at a play the psychological effect of tragedy is one of catharsis, a relieving of powerful emotion by sympathy felt at one remove. For the actors portraying those emotions the effect is nearer, more authentic and internal, with youthful actors more so. For Mary such paralyzing moments, sharpened by personal memory, could not be endured endlessly.

She never acted again, never again set foot on a stage or a movie set. At the young age of twenty-four, smothering her old ambitions, she turned her back permanently and completely on the stage. The brief, bare comment, "I really didn't want to be an actress," was all she ever offered by way of explanation.

For the next fifty years, staying in touch with only a few friends of her youth, she pursued a very private life, living at different times in Mexico, Italy,

Spain, Morocco, and Greece. She traveled much (in *that* she was most like her father), learned to paint, wrote a good deal of poetry, none published, or, it seems, read by anyone else. Her marriage in 1950 to Walter Brooks, stepson of General Douglas MacArthur, lasted a bare seventeen months and ended in divorce (she charged cruelty, a result of her husband's alleged alcoholism).

Three decades of European living passed before she again came back home. By then the family estate, her father's old "ranch" on the ocean shore at Santa Monica, had been donated to the state of California, a loss that saddened her still further, making her feel at last truly "homeless and adrift." While in this country she paid her first and only visit to the Will Rogers Memorial Museum in Claremore. That was in 1981, and the few minutes she spent at her parents' tomb brought only an aching flow of tears.

In 1989 she returned to Los Angeles from Greece for eye surgery. By now she had become friendly with the woman who ran the Will Rogers Memorial Museum in Claremore, Reba Collins. The two women corresponded and, as Ms. Collins recalled, "we talked frequently by phone. We began by exchanging bits of philosophy—about life (how to stay well and enjoy it) and death, when we had to face it. She recommended books for me to read that mixed faith and medicine and love, and we then talked about those, late at night on the phone." Very soon in the friendship Ms. Collins had confirmed for her the widely believed truth about the elderly daughter of Will Rogers, that "she could not shake off the constant reminders of her beloved parent."

Mary's last illness—ovarian cancer—came on while she was still in this country. Ms. Collins visited her briefly toward the end, in December 1989, and recalled a woman by then physically frail and tired of life: "I stayed at her apartment one night during her fatal illness, and stood by her bedside, seeing the pain, telling her I knew she was a winner, not to give up . . . I only wish I could have stayed a little longer—to hold her hand and tell her, finally, that it was OK to let go. She had fought long enough. There was nothing that could keep her frail body alive."

Mary's long, brave fight, Ms. Collins quietly infers, was not only against that last, culminating illness.

THE CRASH AGAIN—WHAT REALLY HAPPENED

A minute-by-minute retelling of the story of the fatal flight as a continuous narrative drawing on all authentic primary sources. Covers the nearly six hours from takeoff at Fairbanks to the tragic finale at Barrow, and adds to what is definitely known those elements of the story that are obvious, necessary, and probable. Not otherwise can those silent six hours in the air, now obscured by death, be filled in, or the crash explained.

15

MOST OF THE SPACE in the cabin of the little red plane as it lifts off from Harding Lake near Fairbanks is taken up with a variety of sacks, bundles, and boxes holding equipment and supplies. Perched on the single seat at the cabin's rear, balancing his old portable typewriter on his knees, Will pecks away two-fingered, writing his next weekly column. It's about the importance of dogs in Alaska. The airplane may have negated travel by dogsled, he writes, "but still the backbone of the Arctic is a dog's backbone."

He's also writing about Joe Crosson's dog, the little terrier, Mickey. He tells how once in camp Mickey bravely attacked a bear, which chased him home, and they had to shoot the bear to save the dog. Smiling to himself, Will taps out the story's conclusion: "An old pet dog jumps a bear . . . an' then they hike straight to you, and the bear after em, and the first thing you know you got the bear in your lap and a dog between your feet . . . so there is two kinds of bear dogs, the ones that drive em away and the ones that brings em in."

Fifteen minutes later Will and Wiley can see the center of Fairbanks down on their left. Then they're passing over the settlements of Heine Creek and Livengood, and barely an hour after that they spot the Yukon River stretching across their path in the distance. Will has put his typewriter aside and turned to the book *Arctic Village*, now his favorite reading. The village it's about, Wiseman, is only another hour ahead, and Will wants to get the flavor of the place. Wiley has agreed that they might go down and stop there for a few hours if everything looks right.

Skipping through the book's almost four hundred pages, Will reads a little in one chapter, then a little in another, and another, selecting those that promise something a bit out of the ordinary: "An Evening at Big Jim's," and "Living Off the Country," and "The Quest for Gold." Two that would certainly have caught his attention are "White Conversation" and "Eskimo Conversation."

Talking loud over the roar of the motor, Wiley shouts that Wiseman is coming up in a few minutes on the right. With that, Will rapidly turns the pages to the book's five-page conclusion. What he reads touches precisely on what has always fascinated him about life in Alaska: that it is somehow different, that the people are different, that it is somehow a special world of its own. In Will's imagination, it seems, Alaska is not unlike the Oklahoma Territory of the 1880s, when he was a boy growing up there:

> . . . the [white] people of the Koyukuk . . . stress their independence as the most precious component in their lives . . . each man has the privilege of working out his own destiny . . . this gives them a buoyant self-reliance, an emancipation from other men's restraints, which immensely enriches the entire pattern of their lives . . . the work is tremendously interesting, and is featured by the lure of the unknown . . .
>
> Any person is free to say anything, read anything, write anything, do anything except commit murder or robbery, and perhaps rape . . . This freedom of thought and action seems to be a genuine incentive to happiness . . . Because there are so few people in the Koyukuk, every person can really feel that he is a vital element in the world in which he lives . . . I believe that the happiness of the Koyukuker, true happiness, is greatly enhanced and his entire life is made richer by the overpowering loveliness of the Arctic wilderness . . . A person misses many things by living in the isolation of the Koyukuk but he gains a life filled with an amount of freedom, tolerance, beauty, and contentment such as few human beings are ever fortunate enough to achieve.

The village of Wiseman as Rogers saw it from the air while looking at this photo of it in the book he was reading, *Arctic Village*. His wish to stop for a visit was overruled by Post.

The view to the east of Wiseman in another photo in *Arctic Village*.

Will puts down the book and sits gazing out the window. Spread below him he sees the very place, the village of Wiseman, that those words were written about. "Wiley!" he calls out excitedly. "That Wiseman, it looks just like this here picture in the book! The image! Let's stop and have us a good look." There's a month of columns down there, he thinks.

The plane's nose dips and the plane begins a slow descent. "We'll see what's what and then decide," replies Wiley. "Need a good spot to land. Not too far away. I'm no good walking, especially in the snow."

"Wiseman's on the Koyukuk River. Should be OK."

When he'd come down to a couple of hundred feet above the ground, Post straightened the plane and headed toward a wide cluster of buildings, the ten-thousand-foot Mt. Doonerak looming beyond them. Minutes later the plane drones over Wiseman's several dozen roofs, lining both sides of the river, drawing upturned faces and vigorous waving from the few people on the ground. Then the plane swings left, heading west along the narrow, twisting river.

"Sorry, Will," shouts Post, finally. "Doesn't look good for a safe landing. Shallow and narrow, and too much current. No lakes near, either. Let's not take a chance. We'll keep going." Not waiting for a reply from his passenger, Wiley puts the plane into a fast climb. Disappointment showing on his face, Will sits staring out the window at the rapidly diminishing village.

(On the stage back at Lakewood, costumed as a stewardess, wearing a brown leather flying jacket, carrying helmet, goggles, and gloves, Mary has just made her entrance.)

"Now come the Endicotts!" laughs Wiley. "This should be fun, trying to find those passes Joe marked on this chart. Just look at all those jagged peaks!" A half hour later the plane enters the wide Anaktuvuk Pass near Chandler Lake. The lower hills of the Brooks Range come next, and then the Colville River appears, a broad, blue ribbon in the distance.

"From here," calls out Wiley, as the land below changes from hills to flat, featureless tundra, strewn with dozens of lakes, "I think we'll skip that business of going up to the coast like Joe said and following it along to Barrow. We're through the mountains now so we can save time and head straight up. We'll use this village"—he points to the chart—"as a signpost. Atkasuk. From there Barrow's a forty-mile hop due north."

Wiley glances at his watch. They'd been in the air some three and a half hours. Another hour or so and they'd be eating reindeer steak at Charlie Brower's table.

It is ten minutes later that the fog begins to close in, at first as stray white wisps, then heavier clumps. Soon it is everywhere, thick, white, and fleecy, enveloping the little red plane. "I think we'd better get down and see what's what," calls out Wiley as he drops the plane's nose. "Looks like there's a good-sized lake over there on the right." Swiftly the plane descends, skimming along the calm silver surface, then touches down, two fine sprays of water kicking up behind the pontoons. For as far as they can see around them there is only the flat, frozen tundra.

Leaving the engine in idle, holding the chart, Post leaves his seat and comes back into the cabin. Will gets up and, hunched over, comes forward.

"I figure we're about here," explains Wiley, tapping a finger on the chart. "And here's Atkasuk. So Barrow's another hundred miles, I guess." Throwing a squinting look up, he adds, "The ceiling here I'd put at a couple hundred feet. The coast near Barrow, on this side of it, to the west, is maybe fifty minutes. If we don't hit Barrow on the nose, we'll fetch up a mile or two west of it. Either way we're in good shape."

He glances at Will. "We could sit here and rest a while, if you want, look around some, maybe see some wildlife . . . but the engine'll cool off and—"

"No. Let's go."

"What about it, Will?" asks Wiley abruptly. "If we go on to Nome from Barrow it'll be time for you to make up your mind. Moscow with me, or home. Thought about it?"

"Yeah, I thought about it . . . y'know I'd like to go . . . dang it, I feel like a deserter already an' I ain't said yes nor no! You know my Mary is up in Maine actin' in that stock company. I'd sure like to keep goin' on with you, but—"

"That's OK, Will. Don't trouble yourself about it. I sorta figured that's what you'd do. Go see your kid doing her stuff on the stage. Mary'd like that. Nobody she respects more than you."

"She's been up there all summer an' I wanted to go see her, told her I'd try . . . y'know, she's awful good . . . I seen her a few times an' I think she can be somebody! A real actor, not like her old Daddy who—"

"Isn't it kinda late to see her on stage? Summer's nearly over. How long do those stock companies go on?"

"Yeah, but I can catch her last few appearances. They keep on till in September sometime. I have her schedule here"—he pulls out a folded piece of paper—"right now, this whole week, she's doin' a play from Broadway they call *Ceiling Zero*. All about flyin' an' how dangerous it is . . . I didn't want her to do that one but—"

"I know about that play. Read about it in the papers. In this business, my business, we don't like it. You can understand. Scares the pants off people with those crashes, the way they do it, you'd think it was a real crash, the papers say. Nobody'll want to fly anymore! But I mean you're safer in a plane than you are in some auto on those crowded highways!"

"That's what I'm sayin'! Here I am practically living in a airplane up here, an' Mary's back east all mixed up with planes crashin'! She didn't like it, neither, but she give in. Said she has to learn to do everything, an' she's right. Anyway, the play's over on Saturday. Next week I can see her in a nice little play called"—he glances at the schedule—"*The Little Inn*. After that she'll do the one called *Rain*, by that Englishman. Of course you know that her mama's up there already . . . Gosh, Wiley, tell me I ain't a deserter!"

Wiley laughs. "Forget it, Will. It's nothing. If I was lucky enough to have a kid like that I'd do the same. Go on and see your kid. Give her and Betty my regards and best wishes. I'll drop you back in Fairbanks after we see Barrow. Then I'll go on to Nome. Joe'll fly you down to Seattle. From there it's only overnight to Maine, with a stop at Chicago."

In the air again, keeping just under the fog, Wiley heads toward the village of Atkasuk. As they fly, the fog drops lower and Wiley descends, trying to get under it, but it follows him, and he goes up, trying to get over it. Even much higher its moist caress clings all round the plane. It hardly mattered. If he escapes the fog by going high, he still won't be able to see the ground, and will have to fly by guess and by feel while hoping for a break, a clearing.

By now at least a half hour of anxious blind flying has passed. To himself Wiley suddenly thinks, We could be out over the ocean! Might have passed the coast and gone out too far. Slowly he banks into a right turn, flies for a

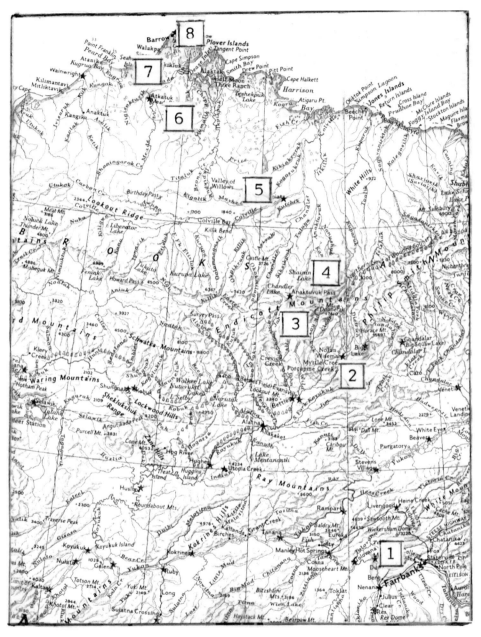

(1) Fairbanks, (2) Village of Wiseman, (3) Endicott Mountains, (4) Anaktuvuk Pass, (5) First halt on unidentified lake, (6) village of Atkasuk, (7) Walakpa, (8) Barrow.

few minutes, then banks right again. No breaks in the fog. No least sign of ground. On he flies, dropping a little, rising again, growing desperate to see some spot of solid earth.

He was right. He *had* been out over the Arctic Ocean, at least fifteen miles out. It was the very situation encountered by the Lindberghs when they were fogbound coming into Barrow four years earlier. "Out to sea the white wall of fog stood impassable," wrote Mrs. Lindbergh of that dangerous moment, "inland under floating islands of fog stretched the barren Arctic land." On and on the Lindberghs flew "through the unreal shifting world of soft mist . . . no sight of land, no sight of sea or sky." The Lindberghs were rescued from their predicament by Sergeant Morgan's telegraph. Wiley might have received similar help from Morgan as to conditions at and around Barrow if he'd been able to work his own radio-telegraph. But even if he could reach it from his pilot's seat, he couldn't send Morse code while flying an unbalanced, nose-heavy plane blind in a pea soup fog.

Now he is heading inland again, passing high over fogbound Smith's Bay, on the coast to the east of Barrow. In his boat on the water below sits the trader Gus Masik. Listening to the sound of the motor overhead, he wonders who it could be flying in such weather—will he try to land? As long as he can hear the droning sound, Masik keeps looking up, but he can see nothing, and soon the motor dies away, going west.

(Back in Maine, on the Lakewood stage, the first of the two crashes in *Ceiling Zero* has just taken place. The shattering sound of it over the loudspeaker reverberates jarringly through the hall, making the audience stir uncomfortably. Mary is on stage for the scene, as played in the airline's office, and she delivers the final line before the crash, shouting an anguished, "Tex! Look Out!")

"Will!" shouts Wiley. "Keep a lookout through the window on your left for a break in the fog. Any sort of clearing big or small! I'm a little hampered on that side. I'll watch on the right. We got to get down! Sing out if you spot anything that even looks like a clearing. Doesn't have to be big. Just so I can get a peek at the ground."

Another twenty minutes go by. In the cabin Will sits with his face pressed to the glass. His eyes are beginning to blur and tear from the effects of staring so constantly at the unbroken whiteness filling all outside. In the plane there is only silence except for the throaty drone of the powerful engine.

"There! There!" shouts Will. "See down there. Near the shore. Is that a tent?"

Wiley takes a quick look, spots land through the small rent in the fog, whispers a fervent thank God, and drops the nose sharply. "Yeah, it's a tent. And there's a man over there by the lagoon. An Eskimo, looks like."

When still fifty feet above the lagoon's surface Wiley notes that its depth is shallow, maybe not even as much as five feet. Can't help that, he thinks as he puts the pontoons gingerly on the water, and throttles down. Skimming along the surface the pontoons twice scrape lightly over submerged sandbars. Near the shore the plane halts and the pontoons settle easily on the water. Wiley lets the engine idle; they won't be staying long. All they want is the distance to Barrow, and which way.

Wearing rubber boots, both men climb out and drop down to the pontoons, then wade the few feet to shore. Smiling, they offer their hands to the Eskimo, who smiles back and shakes each hand in turn.

(On the stage in Lakewood the second airplane crash is minutes away. Over the loudspeaker comes the anxious voice of Humphrey Bogart as Dizzy Davis: "Ice looks a foot thick on the leading edges. I'm down to fifteen hundred feet . . .")

"Speak English?" asks Wiley. "Where *Barrow*? That way?" He stretches an arm out toward the west.

The Eskimo shakes his head and points to the east along the coast. "Barrow there."

"Long way? Many miles?"

"No. Maybe ten. Not many." Looking at the plane, the Eskimo asks, "Why you make plane go up in fog? Bad for plane."

Will laughs. "Bad is right. Go on, Wiley, tell him how we got into this! Well, it don't matter now. We're about there. We'll be at Charlie Brower's place in no time."

"Charlie Brower?" asks the Eskimo. "I know Charlie! He my friend."

"Is that right? Well, ain't that sumpin'. First man we meet in this here frozen wilderness is a—"

"Everybody know Charlie, everbody friend. Charlie big man Barrow."

"That your tent?" asks Will. "You live out here?"

"Live Barrow. Come here hunt. Family in tent."

"What you hunt for? Polar bear?"

The Eskimo laughs. "No bear! No now. Hunt bear sometime with other mans. Hunt seal. Walrus. Caribou."

"Reindeer?"

"Reindeer no wild. Keep in"—he brought his hands together, fingers laced.

"A herd?"

"Yes. Keep in herd."

"The seal and the walrus. Where are they?"

"On ice. There." He points out to sea. "Maybe sometime in water."

"Polar bear, you *like* hunt them sometime? Very dangerous?"

"I like hunt. Bear meat good. Yes, very danger, sometime bear hunt me! Not good! Bad!" The Eskimo makes a face as of a fierce bear, then laughs. Will joins him.

"Have good luck so far? Many seal? Many walrus?"

"Two seal. One walrus. Plenty meat now."

"Come on, Will, let's get going," urges Post. "The ceiling's lifting a bit. Should be OK for the ten miles to Barrow. I'm getting hungry!"

(Over the loudspeaker at Lakewood the voice of Bogart speaks its final anxious words: "Won't answer the controls . . . starting to spin . . . G'bye gang. So long Jake . . .")

Will and Wiley shake hands with the Eskimo, thank him for his help, wade back to the plane, climb up on the wing, and enter the cabin. "Make sure everything's secure," instructs Wiley. "I'll be taking off at a pretty steep angle. Lagoon's big but it's shallow. Don't want to go scraping over a sandbar with a long takeoff run."

In the cockpit, Wiley revs the engine, then turns and taxies out to the middle of the lagoon, bringing the plane's nose around into the slight breeze. His heading is almost due east to Barrow, and a little out to sea. The big engine roars, splitting the chilled quiet of the barren scene. Moments later the plane leaps ahead on the water, fast picking up speed. When there is barely fifty feet of water remaining ahead of it, the plane's nose lifts abruptly into the air, the rising, angled pontoons churning the water behind into a boiling froth.

The plane is airborne.

Up, up it hurtles, the motor humming smoothly and strongly, but as it passes a hundred feet there breaks out the ominous sound of an engine beginning to miss, sputtering badly. In the cockpit, Wiley immediately guesses what has happened: the tank he'd flown in on had gone nearly dry. Looking for a clearing in the fog, he'd forgotten the need to switch tanks. His hand flashes to the lever to make the switch, and almost in the same motion he puts the plane into a sharp right bank, initiating a U-turn.

The two maneuvers, done almost simultaneously, are the actions of a pilot of great skill and presence of mind. If the gas from the new tank fails to flow, or doesn't flow soon enough and fast enough, he'll have to descend powerless, as a glider. But there is only that one lagoon to come down on, and it is now behind him. Already he is far out over the solid tundra, which threatens only disaster for the landing of a pontooned craft. He has to get back over the lagoon.

If the engine catches, he'll be OK. If he has to come down and he's over water, he'll also be OK.

He hadn't calculated on the plane's excessive front-end weight. At two hundred feet, with the motor giving its final cough and suddenly growing silent, the plane entirely loses its upward impetus and noses over—the ground starts coming up fast . . .

"We're going down!" bellows Wiley as he fights to pull the falling plane out of its headlong dive and into a shallower descent for a landing on the water. "Brace yourself!"

The forward tips of the two pontoons hit first, crumpling and tearing as they slice through the water and smack against the lagoon's hard bottom, only four feet down. Next, the stopped, three-bladed propeller smashes against the earth, the blades bending and twisting. As the big engine hits the water it sends up a huge splashing wave, and there bursts out a ragged tongue of flame, marked by a rushing column of thick, black smoke. The nose hits bottom, driving the engine back into the cockpit, and crushing Wiley against the seat.

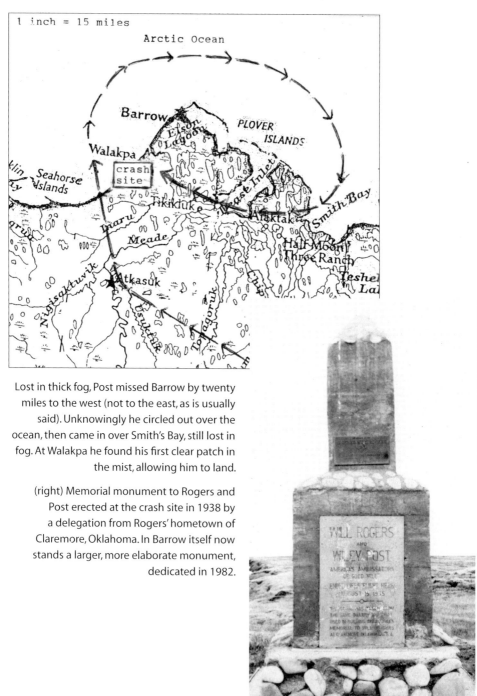

1 inch = 15 miles

Arctic Ocean

Barrow

PLOVER ISLANDS

Elson Lagoon

Walakpa

crash site

Seahorse Islands

Smith Bay

Tikiduke

Meade

Atktak

Half Moon Three Ranch

Teshe Lai

Nigisaktuvik

Atkasuk

Topagoruk

Lost in thick fog, Post missed Barrow by twenty miles to the west (not to the east, as is usually said). Unknowingly he circled out over the ocean, then came in over Smith's Bay, still lost in fog. At Walakpa he found his first clear patch in the mist, allowing him to land.

(right) Memorial monument to Rogers and Post erected at the crash site in 1938 by a delegation from Rogers' hometown of Claremore, Oklahoma. In Barrow itself now stands a larger, more elaborate monument, dedicated in 1982.

WILL ROGERS AND WILEY POST

At the cabin's rear, Will's frantic grasp on the chair arms is torn loose. He is flung forward, along with the piles of baggage, the length of the tilted cabin.

On impact the tail stands up at almost a ninety-degree angle. Then it flops all the way over, sending the thin top edge of the upside-down rudder cutting through the swirling water and into the lagoon bottom. The flames disappear and Will is thrown free of the jumble of debris, coming to rest on the cabin's ceiling, now its wreckage-strewn floor. Around him settle the loose torn bundles of supplies along with his broken typewriter, page three of his last story still in it. (It is possible that the hard-edged typewriter caused Will's fatal head injuries.)

With the cabin resting upside down in the water, Wiley's strapped-in body hangs imprisoned in the inverted seat, his head washed by the fast-rising water.

Some minutes pass. Then from outside the wrecked plane comes an excited shouting, a string of Eskimo words yelled loudly over and over. At last, after some five minutes the shouting stops. Now all is peaceful, with only the low hiss of the hot engine cooling in the water to be heard, and the forlorn cries of the few seagulls that come wheeling over the wreck.

In her dressing room at Lakewood, Mary finishes changing, then smiles a good night to the other girls, and leaves the theater. Outside, the air is comfortably warm and the quarter moon is bright. Well before she reaches the cottage, the blaring of the loudspeaker has ceased to echo in her head. By now it's getting to be old stuff, she realizes. Still jarring, yes, but a really great piece of theater.

Today the Walakpa Lagoon area looks and feels about the same as it did in 1935. Except in the eyes of the Eskimos, to whom it is familiar ground, it is still barren and starkly desolate, still swept by the icy winds forever blowing in off the Arctic Ocean. One conspicuous difference is the tall stone-and-concrete memorial standing on the shore near the crash site. It was built on the spot, in 1938, by friends of Will Rogers from Claremore. The stones were brought all the way from Oklahoma—by boat from Seattle to Barrow—and the concrete was mixed right there using water from the lagoon.

When it was finished and erected, those good friends from Claremore, joined by Barrow's Eskimo choir from the Presbyterian church and a bunch of other folks from the village including the Greists, the Morgans, the Daughertys, the Browers, and the Okpeahas, had a little dedication ceremony. There was some very nice choir singing, and a speech or two. Then they unveiled the monument. It reads:

WILL ROGERS

and

WILEY POST

America's Ambassadors

of Good Will

Ended Life's Flight Here

August 15, 1935

Notes and Sources

—————— ≋✦≋ ——————

Only items directly related to the book's main focus are individually cited, including of course all quoted matter. For the background of Rogers' life I rely on the biographies by Croy, Robinson, Mrs. Rogers, and Yagoda. The pioneer effort to recover the full story of the fatal crash itself is Sterling, *Death* (1993). Sources are given in shortened form and may be identified by a glance at the Bibliography. Reconstructed dialogue in quotes is designated *dial. recon.* All else in quotes is verbatim from the source. Down the left-hand margin are page numbers.

3   "Will Rogers, accustomed": *Cleveland Plain Dealer,* August 17, 1935.

10   *Clarence Badger visit:* In 1957 Badger wrote out his reminiscences of Rogers, including a detailed account of his visit in July 1935, fifteen days before the fatal flight (original manuscript at the Eastman House, Rochester, N.Y. It was first published in Sterling, *Hollywood,* 8–16). My account of the visit reasonably expands on what Badger states or clearly implies.

11   *The Emerson verse:* From the long poem *Monadnoc.*

11   "He sent the poor man": *Oregonian,* September 1, 1935, article by Mabel Merrick. Rogers' "technique," of course, was merely being himself, wonderfully relaxed and offhand.

11   "I shot the car through": Sterling, *Hollywood,* 16. Same for the other Badger quotes, verbatim or *dial. recon.*, 16–19.

12   "As I mounted the": Sterling, *Will Rogers in Hollywood*, 9. Same for the next Badger quote.

14   *The Roosevelt fan letter:* Facsimile in Sterling, *Hollywood*, 149. Roosevelt often declared himself to be WR's "good friend" and sincere admirer, as did Wilson. Coolidge and Harding both liked him—they could hardly say otherwise!—but both proved a little touchy about his good-humored jibes.

15   *Badger reference to the Alaska trip:* Sterling, *Hollywood,* 16 (verbatim and *dial. recon.*). WR's closing quote: Sterling, *Hollywood*, 16.

15   *Background of the planned flight:* The day's newspapers and Sterling, *Death*, 116–17. Discussion touched *where* they were going, and *why.*

18   "We took a long ride": Rogers, *Wife's Story,* 304. Also 11–12 for the next two quotes.

19   "Don't go, Will, please": *Richmond Times-Dispatch,* August 17, 1935. An AP release, the short item appeared boxed on many front pages.

19   "Will Rogers will not": *San Francisco Chronicle,* August 8, 1935. Actually, he did not make up his mind about Russia until near the end of the Alaska trip, in fact while on his way to Barrow.

22   *Alterations to the plane*: These were much discussed in the newspapers after the accident (August 17–20, 1935, and September 4–6, 1935), especially regarding the big new engine, and the pontoons. For a round-up view, see Sterling, *Eagle,* 164–68, 175–79.

23   "No one ever wrote so": Rogers, *Wife's Story,* 291. WR did have quite a facility as a ready writer, of course, because he didn't so much compose as simply write down a form of spontaneous *talk,* unpolished and unrevised, as readers then liked it.

24   "He's a marvelous flyer": *San Francisco Chronicle,* August 6, 1935. Rogers made the same remarks about Post many times.

25   "He could take off": O'Brien, 21, and Sterling, *Death*, 119. The comment, probably by Crosson, was offhand, no more than a casual remark, and in no way implied approval. As with all experienced Alaska pilots, Crosson understood that flying with pontoons required a gentler touch.

26   *Skipping Ketchikan*: That this was Post's idea is my own conclusion. Ketchikan as a destination is mentioned by WR in several news stories at the time. See Sterling, *Eagle,* 189. *Dial. recon.*

27   *Joe Crosson in Juneau: New York Times,* August 8, 1935; Tordoff, 182–83. *Dial. part recon.* Crosson background: Tordoff, *Mercy Pilot,* passim.

30   "The happiest civilization": Marshall, *Village,* dedication.

32   *Meeting with Rex Beach*: A lengthy account by Beach himself appeared in many papers after the crash. See *Washington Post,* August 18, 1935; also Collins, *Crash,* 27.

33   "Goin' to Skagway": Collins, *Crash*, 10, quoting a Rogers column.

34   *Visit to Aklavik: Washington Post*, August 13, 1935; Collins, *Crash*, 12–13; Sterling, *Death,* 142–43 (a photo following p. 143 shows Rogers with a Russian government official).

35   *Barrow and its white families*: The most helpful primary sources are Brower's own book, *Fifty Years Below Zero*; his diary (original at Rasmuson Library, University of Alaska Fairbanks); the various issues of Dr. Greist's newsletter, *The Northern Cross* (issues at Dartmouth and University of Alaska Fairbanks); Greist's unpublished autobiography, *Seventeen Years with the Eskimo* (copies at Dartmouth and University of Alaska Fairbanks); Anne Morrow Lindbergh's *North to the Orient*, 95–110; and O'Brien, 227–29. Neither Morgan nor Daugherty left any writings on their experience of life in Barrow. Helpful is Lyn Kidder's guide, *Barrow from A to Z* (1995).

36   "an old Scotch whaleman": Lindbergh, 104. This was probably the A. H. Hopson mentioned in *Northern Cross* (August 1935, 21) as "a typical Englishman of the old school." The same issue lists his death in the flu epidemic that year.

36   "to check upon our": Greist, *Northern Cross*, August 1935, 23. The quote occurs in a long and interesting article about "The Epidemic of Influenza" that hit Alaska's northern slope that spring. Greist makes clear the difficulties of caring for an Eskimo population with inadequate diet and little faith in medical procedure: "Any attempt to intelligently practice medicine among them, if he be a competent physician and dictician, he will tear his hair and declare in the end that the situation is impossible . . . 'tis useless to issue orders and leave them within the home [their igloos]—orders are remembered only until the doctor leaves." Evident is Greist's concern for, and even love of, his Native charges.

37   "The Fourth was celebrated": Greist, *Northern Cross*, August 1935, 27.

37   *The Greist house*: Lindbergh, 101; *Northern Cross*, June 1930, 44–45.

41   *Gray wolves at Barrow: Northern Cross*, January 1934, 54.

41   *Crosson and the Morris children: Northern Cross*, August 1933, 17.

42   *Greist on ice floe: Northern Cross*, March 1934, 6.

42   "We can show as good": Greist, *Northern Cross*, August 1933, 18.

43   "Out to sea the white": Lindbergh, 95–98; also 99–107.

45   *Brower absent*: Brower, *Fifty*, 293–94.

46   "Morgan hurried over": Brower, *Fifty*, 295. He adds that "no plane appeared that day or next. When a spell of particularly bad weather followed, with snow and sleet and no visibility whatever, we resigned ourselves to an indefinite postponement . . . We'd seldom experienced a meaner storm. At times you couldn't see fifty yards." The "vile" weather on the fifteenth and for several days, is confirmed in Brower's letter to Bernet later that year: on the fifteenth there had been "no

visibility and no ceiling—just dense fog that one had to shove aside to get through." It was raining and "at times there were snow squalls." This firsthand testimony invalidates claims by a few that Barrow weather on the fifteenth was more or less clear.

46 *The gathering at Crosson's apartment*: Tordoff, 185, *dial. recon.* The information came from Lillian herself, including the fact that they talked of going to Barrow, meeting Brower, and Joe's offer to fly them up. My picture expands on Tordoff, using known fact. Also, 2008 interview of Lillian Crosson.

47 "Almost went to Barrow": Collins, *Crash*, 12, quoting a WR column.

48 *WR wires Brower*: Brower, *Fifty*, 295, where Brower records his receiving the telegram, though not quoting it. The actual wire no longer exists—it is not among the Brower papers at the University of Alaska Fairbanks.

48 *Visit to Matanuska*: Contemporary newspapers gave the event wide coverage. See Collins, *Crash*, 13–17, and Ketchum, 273–74. That the government article on Matanuska was prompted by the WR column is my own conclusion, a safe one, I feel.

50 "He was very sentimental": Tordoff, 186.

51 *The telegram*: Collins, *Crash*, 59.

53 *Fueling the plane at Harding Lake*: Tordoff, 186, Sterling, *Death*, 161, 164–66. There was confusion about this operation, some papers reporting that Post put down at Harding to wait out the bad weather, an error that crept into later accounts.

53 *Post's failure to phone*: Tordoff, 187; Sterling, *Eagle*, 228–29. This omission on Post's part was his most serious and inexcusable lapse, hard to explain. To ignore the warnings of experienced pilots about the hazards of Alaska weather, when the information was ready to hand, was the act of a daring but sometimes foolhardy nature. It could only have resulted from the impatience and sense of hurry that had gripped Post from the start. Dirk Tordoff, Crosson's biographer, and a man particularly knowledgeable as to Alaska flying, wrote that the Rogers-Post crash was "one of the most tragic and avoidable incidents in Alaska aviation history . . . Alaska's past and future will be forever dotted with tragic examples of pilots who through ignorance or arrogance took to the air when they should have remained on firm ground. Even more sadly, the accounts invariably include trusting passengers who accompanied these airmen to their doom . . . Will Rogers was one such passenger . . . Rogers' faith in Post was taken to the grave" (*Alaska History*, Spring 1995, review of Sterling, *Death at Barrow*).

54 *The Lakewood Theater*: Basic information comes from the book *Bringing Broadway to Maine*, by John Oblak; the *Somerset Reporter* (Maine weekly), May–September, 1934–36; and the *New York Times*, June 23, 1935.

54   "You're right, this idea": Mary to her father, November 1933, original at the Will Rogers Memorial Museum, Claremore. She continues: "I have had no experience whatever except silly school plays. I thought that before I contemplate any real acting I should have some coaching. Paula and Carol take from a wonderful dramatic teacher who taught Ina Claire, Katharine Hepburn, Connie Bennett, loads of people. I would like to have some work with her & get the feel of things & maybe at the same time get a small walk on-walk off in some show in New York—just for the experience of being before an audience—maybe only speaking one line or nothing much at all." Her acting ambitions, however, still had to contend with her strong family feeling. She adds: "If you are not going to work this summer & are going some place I do wish there was some way we could all go together. It would be about the last chance of our getting to travel together. That's the part I'd hate of working this summer. It would mean not being with you and mother & it does seem rather hard to be away all winter & summer too . . . Goodnight Darling—its getting late and I must go to bed. Do write to me when you have a spare minute—its wonderful hearing from you . . . heard you at the premier of Cavalcade you were grand wish I could have been there."

54   "A stock company in": WR to Mary, November 1933, original at the Will Rogers Memorial Museum, Claremore.

55   "How's my little actress": WR to Mary, November 1934, original at the Will Rogers Memorial Museum, Claremore.

55   "You got your old": WR to Mary, a telegram, January 14, 1935. Original at the Will Rogers Memorial Museum, Claremore.

55   "clever" and "brilliant": *Bangor Daily News*, August 12, 1935.

55   "Mary is just one of": *Somerset Reporter*, August 18, 1935.

55   "a beautiful, controlled": Collins, *Leader*.

56   *Ceiling Zero*: It ran at Lakewood August 12–17. By then Mary had appeared in ten of Lakewood's first dozen offerings. I am assuming that Mary would, even beforehand, have been uncomfortable about appearing in a plane-disaster production while her father was spending most of his days in the air. More sensitive casting might have given Mary's part to some other Lakewood actress—but probably by the time WR's plans were known it was too late to make changes. The following year the play was made into a movie, with Cagney in the Bogart role.

56   *Humphrey Bogart*: He came to Lakewood late that summer directly from his hit Broadway performance in *Petrified Forest* (the following year, a film starring Bogart, Leslie Howard, and Bette Davis). At the time, his rise to screen fame had barely begun.

56   "in a new plane he": *Somerset Reporter*, June 21, 1935.

58   "There is truly a": *New York Times*, June 23, 1935, as quoted in Oblak, 97. Oblak adds, "At the time a member of the Lakewood company was receiving $45 a week and paying his own room and board . . . the outdoor recreational attraction, as always, was the 'supplemental income' Lakewood could offer."

59   *Weather reports from Barrow*: Brower, *Fifty*, 295, Brower letter to Bernet, in Collins, *Crash*, 34.

59   "was a busy but routine": Brower, *Fifty*, 295.

60   *Okpeaha reaches Barrow*: Daugherty, *New York Herald-Tribune*, August 17, 1935; Brower, unpublished diary, August 15, 1935, 78; Brower, *Fifty*, 297; *Northern Cross*, November 1935. *Dial. part recon.* Sterling (*Death*, 183, and *Eagle*, 245–46) gives a slightly different picture of Okpeaha's arrival in Barrow. He has the Eskimo going straight to Brower's house, not to Daugherty, and encountering Brower's son Tom, to whom he first tells the news of the crash. But this sequence is based on an interview many years later (1986) with Tom Brower. Contemporary testimony of both Brower and Greist make it certain that Okpeaha first roused Daugherty, and was then sent to Brower's house. Okpeaha's broken English, including his use of "mans" for "men": Greist in *Northern Cross*, November 1935.

61   "there came a sharp": Brower, *Fifty*, 296–97.

62   *Morgan's part*: Described by Morgan himself in his lengthy telegram of August 16, widely reprinted by the newspapers. See Collins, *Crash*, 32. Same for next Morgan quote.

63   "not even notified of": Greist, *Northern Cross*, November 1935. Of course, the failure to take the only doctor available to the crash site *does* seem strange. No reason was given for the omission, beyond what Brower said.

63   "a rag on his sore eye,": Greist, *Northern Cross*, November 1935, 36.

64   *The Okpeaha family*: In the tent were Mrs. Okpeaha and her five children, Sadie, Rose, Robert, Fred, and William (all now deceased). Hearing the plane land, all came out to look, watched as it took off again, and saw it crash. In Barrow still live several Okpeaha grandchildren.

68   "a murky fog": Daugherty, *New York World-Telegram*, August 17, 1935.

68   "dense fog and": Morgan in Collins, *Crash*, 32.

69   *Inspecting the wreck*: Based on the accounts of Daugherty in *New York Herald-Tribune* and *New York World-Telegram*, August 17, 1935, and Morgan, in Collins, *Crash*, 32. More is implied in these sources than is clearly stated, permitting considerable expansion. The fact that Rogers' body was not found in the wreck (because it had been moved to the far shore by Natives) *must* have puzzled the two rescuers, as I show. This has not before been realized. *Dial. part recon.*

71   *Mary's entrance speech*: Wead, 20.

72   *The first crash*: Wead, 100–1.

72   "a terrific, metallic": Wead, 101.

72   "One of the most exciting": Quoted in Wead, 141.

72   "at the end of the second": Quoted in Wead, 141.

74   *The second crash*: Wead, 133.

74   *Timing of fictional and real crashes*: In the narrative I place the two crashes fairly close in time, a matter of minutes. The interval may actually have been closer to a half hour. The uncertainty arises because the exact clock times of the two crashes, stage and real, must be calculated, so can be only approximate. An eight p.m. curtain at Lakewood is stated in all the ads, and the approximate running time for *Ceiling Zero* can be calculated from the published script as two and a half hours plus. Between Skowhegan in Maine and Barrow in Alaska, the time-zone difference (not the actual difference) is today four hours. When the play's first crash occurred, at close to 10:30 p.m., up at Barrow it was 6:30, more or less. The second crash is calculated at say a half hour after the first, depending on the pace set by the play's director. Thus the play's second crash is timed to about 11:00, which at Barrow would be 7:00, more or less. The best estimate of the time of the real crash is that given by Sergeant Morgan, about 7:30. One of Okpeaha's daughters later said it happened a little after the family in the tent had eaten supper, which she explained was always about seven (Sterling, *Eagle*, 245, 253). In 1935, before the redrawing of the Alaska time zones in 1983, the difference between Barrow and Lakewood was given as five hours. The change, of course, did not affect the true "physical" difference, which depends on the actual mileage between the two places. A time zone gives the same time for all locations within its borders, but the true local, or "sun time," for all locations varies along an east-west line.

    At first there was confusion as to the actual time of the Walakpa crash because Post's watch was reported as stopped at 8:18. But in that case Okpeaha would have left Walakpa on his two-hour run about 9:00 p.m., much too late to reach Barrow at 10 p.m., as Morgan recorded. Post's watch stopped well after the crash, perhaps by being water-soaked.

75   "That part about Nome": Rogers, *Wife's Story*, 307.

76   *Arrival of Miles and Bogart*: Rogers, *Wife's Story*, 307, which, curiously, mentions only Miles, but see the notes below.

76   "Nothing. Not a thing": The puzzlement of the two at not finding Rogers in or near the wreck, dead or alive, has been overlooked, but is evident in the sources. The conversation (*dial. recon.*) flows necessarily from the fact of their puzzlement, as also their actions. Daugherty's idea about the body being thrown clear is in the *New York Herald Tribune*, August 17, 1935. Rogers' body being found through Okpeaha's son is my own conclusion, and necessary in the circumstances.

78   *Freeing Post's body*: Brower, *Fifty*, 300, and Brower's letter to Bernet, see Collins, *Crash*, 34. Brower says that the pontoons were ripped off the plane entirely, but the photos show that they were simply shifted out of the way.

78   "Dave and I had to": Lavrakas, "Sad Day."

79   "upon the high veranda": Greist, *Seventeen*, 290.

79   "a glance at the two": Brower, *Fifty,* 297.

82   *Preparation of the bodies*: Greist, *Northern Cross*, November 1935; Croy, 303–5 (quoting Greist); Brower, *Fifty*, 298; and the Brower diary, 79.

83   "Not in many years," Greist, *Northern Cross*, November 1935, 35, 37.

84   *Gus Masik*: Brower diary, 80 and Greist, *Northern Cross*, November 1935. Masik was an early trader-adventurer in Alaska. See *Alaska Journal*, winter 1983, 2–16, for his part in an interesting expedition of 1931.

85   "She doubled over as": The words are Bogart's own, taken down during a 1952 interview on the subject of how the news of Rogers' death was received at Lakewood. The interview was conducted by Hollywood publicity agent Bill Blowitz on behalf of Homer Croy, then writing his biography of Rogers. It took place on the set of a Bogart film then in production, *Battle Circus*. Blowitz sent Croy a page and a half of typed notes quoting Bogart in some detail (some of it not quite accurate). The original with cover letter to Croy is at the University of Missouri, Columbia, Homer Croy papers, Ellis Library. (The first use of the information was made in *The Papers of Will Rogers*, vol. 4, A. Wertheim, ed., 409.)

My picture of all that happened that morning in Lakewood reasonably combines the facts supplied by Betty (*Wife's Story*, 307–8), the Bogart interview, the Owen Davis autobiography, and a variety of newspaper accounts, particularly those of the *Somerset Reporter* and the *Bangor Daily News*, August 17–19, 1935. For instance, the Davis claim (p. 129) that it was he who told the news to Betty no doubt only reflects the fact that he hurried to the cottage that morning, that he was on hand as she was told, and offered his sympathy and encouragement. Croy in his account of that moment (p. 307) relies entirely on Betty's version—which obviously makes no attempt to be either detailed or complete—but he confuses Carlton Miles with the Lakewood actor Grant Mills. In Croy, for whatever reason, Bogart gets no mention.

The Blowitz notes have Bogart being fairly circumstantial in his statement, though some needed detail has evidently been skipped. He happened to be in the theater that morning—he says "the box office"—and answered the phone:

> Alaska was calling and wanted to talk with Mrs. Rogers. I told them I would take the message. I was dumbfounded. Then I half walked, half ran the two blocks down the village street to the

cottage in which Mary and Mrs. Rogers were staying. I told Mrs. Rogers that Will was dead. I don't even remember what I said. She doubled up for a minute as though I had hit her. Then she straightened up. I was young and I was tremendously impressed. "Well," she said, "there's a lot of work to be done." [He was actually thirty-five, and Betty's recovery didn't happen as quickly as all that.]

I imagine she told Mary because none of us in the company had an opportunity after that to do more than pat Mary on the shoulder and mumble our sorrow.... Then I went back to the box-office and the telephone. Lindbergh called in and asked to talk to Mrs. Rogers. To my memory, this was the only phone call she actually accepted. [True: Lindbergh offered to fly into Lakewood and take Betty and Mary home to California, along with any other assistance needed. Mary refused to fly and they went home by train.] For the rest of them we took messages....

Telegrams had started to arrive in the little village five miles away. Keenan Wynn, and I went with him occasionally, shuttled back and forth bringing messages—more than 5000 I'm sure.... Mary and Mrs. Rogers didn't leave that same night. The next morning we drove them a couple of stops down the line and they boarded the train out [not the next morning but that same evening, the sixteenth, though he is right about them going by car to an out-of-the-way station "down the line"—Oakland, near Waterville—a move made to avoid the crowds that had begun to gather].... Mrs. Rogers was a tower of strength. Mary seemed stunned....

Just who it was that Bogart talked with in Alaska is not known. Most probably it was longtime family friend Rex Beach, calling from Juneau. If not Beach, then Crosson in Fairbanks, before he left for his flight to Barrow on the sixteenth. It could not have been anyone in Barrow, for there were no phone lines that far north.

86   "I ran after them": Rogers, *Wife's Story*, 307–8. She mentions neither Bogart nor Davis, only Carlton Miles. But her account is curiously brief, and is obviously incomplete. For instance she does not even say how or by whom her daughter was given the news. She also omits the moment she herself was told, implying that it was done by her sister, though this is not at all clear.

86   *Telling Mary*: Davis, 129–31, and *Somerset Reporter*, August 18, 1935. Davis writes that he heard about Rogers' death "by telephone from the press rooms in Portland [Me.] and it had to be broken to Mrs. Rogers and to Mary. A number of times in my life I have had to be the bearer of news like this and I had often

wondered if there wasn't some better way of doing it than the awkward phases I used." His confusion as he looked back is quite natural, mistaking whatever condolences he expressed to Betty, for his being the first bearer of the bad news. He also a little built up his part in getting the three women to the train when they left Lakewood: "The crowd about the cottage where the Rogers were living was growing all the time. . . . I took advantage of the fact that it was night by now and I smuggled Mary and Mrs. Rogers out of their back door and drove them across country to a distant railroad station." Also certainly in on the move were Bogart and Carlton Miles. Davis is right, of course, when he mentions a long drive to "a distant" station.

86   "Mrs. Rogers was on the": *Somerset Reporter*, August 18, 1935.

88   "gently aiding the girl": *Bangor Daily News*, August 19, 1935.

88   "remained in seclusion": *Somerset Reporter*, August 18, 1935.

88   "They would see nobody": *Bangor Daily News*, August 17, 1935.

88   "What will be Mary's": *Somerset Reporter*, August 18, 1935.

89   *Ceiling Zero not canceled*: *Bangor Daily News*, August 17, 1935.

105   *Crosson to Barrow*: Tordoff, *Mercy Pilot*, 189–93 and Lillian Crosson in 2008 interview. The opening scene, as also the entire chapter, develops the information in these and other sources as noted.

107   *Murray Hall*: Sterling, *Death*, 278–89.

108   "Joe was trying to do": Tordoff, *Mercy Pilot*, 191. He adds: "Crosson was really feeling the strain. Throughout the flight he hadn't spoken aloud about the crash or admitted the reason for the trip. It was as if he couldn't admit out loud that his friends were dead."

108   *Crosson in Barrow*: No record exists of the eight or so hours that the two men laid over in Barrow (*Northern Cross*, November 1935 has only a brief paragraph). It is my own conclusion that Crosson viewed the bodies, talked with the others about the circumstances of the crash, closely questioned Okpeaha, and decided not to visit the wreck after viewing photos of it. *Dial. recon*. Rogers' copy of *Arctic Village* is at the museum in Claremore.

110   *Questioning Okpeaha*: The content of the questioning is based on all available sources regarding the accident (*dial. recon.*). The presence of fire in the wreck is mentioned in Daugherty, *New York Herald-Tribune*, August 17, 1935, and Brower's diary, 78.

114   "a forlorn little group": *Oregonian*, August 18, 1935.

120   *The flight from Fairbanks to Seattle*: Tordoff, *Mercy Pilot*, 192–93, and many newspapers, August 19, 1935.

121   *The funeral*: The fullest accounts reporting countrywide observances are in Sterling, *Death*, 290–316, and Collins, *Crash*, 50–89, drawing on the day's voluminous newspaper reports.

122   "Through miles of sun": *Cleveland Plain Dealer*, August 23, 1935. The article was syndicated and appeared in many papers.

123   "There are many echoes": *San Francisco Chronicle*, August 23, 1935.

123   "For some minutes there": *San Francisco Chronicle*, August 23, 1935.

128   *The government accident report*: Published in most papers, often with a different emphasis, on September 4, 1935. See for instance *New York Times*, *Los Angeles Times*, *Chicago Tribune*, *Seattle Post-Intelligencer*, *Minneapolis Pioneer Press*, etc., etc. Sterling, *Death*, 317–54, supplies an extended analysis of the report, at times rather too critical of the authorities. See also Collins, *Crash*, 36–37.

129   "I don't know much about": *Seattle Post-Intelligencer*, as quoted in Sterling, *Death*, 297.

129   "then came the problem of": Post, *Around the World*, 34–35.

130   "to the engine having": Quoted in Collins, *Crash*, 37. Same for the next quote about moisture.

131   *Theory of empty gas tanks*: Okpeaha's eyewitness description of the sputtering and at last silent engine made this an obvious possibility. But the six hours (at most) that the plane was airborne could not have exhausted 270 gallons of gas (about 30 gallons per hour of consumption). Brower added to the confusion when he stated that when his son Dave first arrived at the wreck, he found "not only did none of the tanks contain so much as a drop of gas, but there was no sign of any on the surface of the lagoon" (Brower, *Fifty*, 300). Dave could not have known that there were six tanks aboard, five lacking gauges, and that two of them were in the sheared-off right wing, then lying flat underwater.

131   "with which he was wholly": *New York Herald-Tribune*, August 17, 1935.

131   "he was a careful flyer": *Cleveland Plain Dealer*, August 20, 1935.

132   "sent 25 men two": Brower diary, 81. This same entry contains his reference to Post's quickly at the last moment switching off the engine to avoid fire (p. 82). He also provides some information about the engine itself:

> . . . after communicating with Pratt and Whitney of Hartford, Conn. who owned the engine I have cleaned and packed the same to be shipped to them this coming summer. It was certainly some job taking this engine apart and reassembling it. The engine a Wasp was new and it is surprising to find that after the smashing she must

have had that the working parts are in such good condition, all
the outer parts are broken and gone beyond repair nevertheless all
parts have been cleaned and are now cased for going out. I found
that all the larger parts after reassembling seemed to work perfectly . . . In taking the engine to pieces we found all the cylinders full
of sand also the timing gear as well as most every other part. All the
alloy metal has been badly corroded and eaten by salt water . . .

134   *Disposal of the wreck*: Brower, *Fifty*, 299, Sterling, *Death*, 300. The instrument
      panel was repaired and reinstalled in the *Winnie Mae*, which had been bought
      by the government and put on exhibit at the Smithsonian, where it can still
      be seen.

135   "an ear-splitting fandango": *New York Times*, October 24, 1935.

135   "Mad, merry, melodramatic": *New York World-Telegram*, October 24, 1935.

136   *Mary in* Three Wise Fools: *New York Times*, January 13, 1936. Her going to a
      New Jersey stage I take to be deliberate, since the columns mention her as possi-
      ble for four new Broadway shows: *An American Tragedy*, *Answer Me That*, *Spring
      Dance*, and *Icebound* (by Owen Davis), all scheduled for Broadway production in
      January, February 1936.

136   *nervous breakdown*: See the next note. Since the breakdown occurred in January
      while she was appearing in *Three Wise Fools*, I assume that some signs of it were
      evident toward the close of *Crime*, perhaps even more serious than I suggest.

137   "Mary Rogers, easily the": *Somerset Reporter*, April 2, 1936. The paper's so openly
      and casually referring to Mary's "breakdown" as a fact shows that it was fairly
      common knowledge, at least among theater folk. I have found no other published
      mention of it.

138   "My Dear Daughter. My!": WR to Mary, May 18, 1932, original at the Will
      Rogers Memorial Museum, Claremore. A year later he wrote her another birth-
      day letter, which she may also have reread in those sad days immediately after the
      funeral. In part it reads:

        Dear Old Lady Rogers.

        Why I never thought I would live to be complimenting you
        reaching such a ripe old age . . . How does it feel to leave your teens
        behind, maby this getting old will help your mother and I out, maby
        every time we are kinder against you going or doing something all
        we could hear, Do you realize I am not a child anymore . . . well,
        maby you wont brag on it now. Well, dear, even if you are all grown

up and a fine girl, you are still Daddy's baby girl, you wont mind that will you, Daddy is mighty proud of you, and you have never given me any cause to feel otherwise . . .

It seems funny writing to a grown young lady, why dear this is the first love letter I have written to a young lady in years and years, but it is a love letter and I am in love with you, and hope you are happy and fine, and you will hurry home and see me.

Love and kisses from Old Dad.

141   "The charming lass whose": *Somerset Reporter*, May 21, 1936, which mentions her traveling by boat through the canal. Same for the next quote of Mary.

141   *Mary's brother Will: Somerset Reporter*, August 20, 1936. His staying at Lakewood only four days, centered on the fifteenth, tells its own story as to why he was there.

142   *The August 15 performance*: No special mention of this was made in print that I can find. I take that to mean that all went well.

142   "a record for a feminine": *Somerset Reporter*, September 17, 1936, photo caption. See also *New York Times*, September 18, 1936.

142   *Gordon and Goetz: Somerset Reporter*, August 20, 1936. That the two were there to judge Mary's screen potential is my own conclusion.

142   *The 20th Century Fox movie contract*: Correspondence between Fox and Mrs. Rogers and her lawyers during November 1936–August 1937 at the Will Rogers Memorial Museum, Claremore. *The Last Slaver* went unproduced.

143   "is ill and will be": J. K. Blake to Fox executive A. E. Maynard, January 9, 1937 (Claremore). The illness is nowhere identified.

143   "because of illness": J. K. Blake to Fox executive A. E. Maynard, February 4, 1937, (Claremore).

143   "I really didn't want": Collins, *Leader.*

144   *Mary's subsequent life*: The sources are not plentiful, only *The Papers of Will Rogers*, ed. Wertheimer, vol. 4, 406–10, the Collins 1990 article "Will Rogers' Daughter Mary" in *Oologah Lake Leader*, and a thin Mary Rogers file at the Will Rogers Museum, Claremore. Her marriage and divorce are noted in *New York Times*, September 30, 1950, and March 6, 1952. A brief obituary of only seventeen lines appeared in *New York Times*, December 14, 1989. Obituaries in the California papers are not much more informative.

144   "we talked frequently": Collins, *Leader.* Same for the other quotes from Collins.

147   "but still the backbone": Croy, 311, which gives the article, from Rogers' original
       manuscript. Today only page 3 is still preserved (at Claremore). The full text is
       also given in Collins, *Crash*, 18–19.

147   "An old pet dog jumps": Croy, 313, quoting from the original.

148   "the [white] people of": Marshall, *Village*, 375–76. A photo of Wiseman from
       the air is the book's frontispiece. The Rogers-Post exchange is *dial. recon.*, as is
       most of the conversation in this final section.

150   *The Endicotts*: The description of the flight here is my own conclusion (*dial.
       recon.*).

150   "I think we'll skip": The circumstances of the crash indicate that Post missed
       Barrow by flying *west* of it, not east, as is thought. Thus he must simply have ig-
       nored Crosson's explicit directions. If he had missed it to the east, and flown past
       or over it going west, the sound of his motor (very rare in that locality) would
       surely have been heard by the villagers. But no such claim ever arose. I think he
       missed his target to the west, circled out through the fog over the Arctic Ocean,
       came back over Smith's Bay (east of Barrow), where the drone of the motor *was*
       heard by Gus Masik, flew inland several miles, then circled back toward the west,
       found a rent in the fog over Walakpa, and happily landed on the lagoon. See map,
       p. 153.

151   *The halt near Atkasuk*: This stop I find to be very probable in the circumstances,
       though beyond proof. When first encountering the heavy fog, Post certainly
       would have landed to rethink his situation, as he said at the start of the flight
       that he would. His fatal error, of course, was in deciding to continue north, brav-
       ing the fog, instead of waiting where he was for the fog to clear, which would
       certainly have been done by any experienced Alaska pilot. Post's impatience and
       overconfidence goaded him into a last fatal error of judgment.

151   *Rogers deciding for Maine*: He is on record as telling Mary that he'd try to get up
       to Lakewood before her season ended (*Somerset Reporter*, June 2, 1935, which
       quotes a telegram from WR to Mary on the opening of the 1935 season: ". . . I
       will be up to see you but not until the snow starts melting"). I prefer to believe
       he would have chosen his daughter over Siberia, especially since he showed no
       particular interest in the longer flight planned by Post.

152   *The right turn before the crash*: Post has frequently been criticized for this ma-
       neuver as putting an increased and unnecessary strain on the engine and control
       surfaces, seriously interfering with his frantic effort to level the plane for a land-
       ing. But it has been forgotten that the plane, with its pontoon landing gear, was
       headed away from the lagoon, out over the tundra, hard ground. He *had* to get
       back over water. He could have gone to the left, trying for the ocean. The lagoon
       was closer, and calmer.

160   *The little monument*: Croy, 317–18, which supplies a description by one of the participants. The *New York Times*, August 14, 1938, took note of the dedication ceremony, small but peculiarly solemn.

Added Note
Lillian Crosson
(see pages 46, 105–7)

The beautiful Lillian is still very much alive and still beautiful at age 100. She now lives in Washington State, and my lengthy phone talk with her shows how sharp and strong is her memory of Will Rogers and Wiley Post in the days before they left Fairbanks on that last fatal flight. The morning they left she served them breakfast: Norwegian pancakes. She recalls especially the complaints of friends and neighbors that she didn't throw a party so they could all meet the famous visitors (both preferred not, she said). The shock and horror felt by all on the morning when news of the crash reached them is also still vivid. On Joe's return from Barrow with the two bodies, she was at Fairbanks' Chena River where the pontooned plane set down, watched by a huge, silent crowd. She saw the wrapped bodies as they were transferred from the plane to an undertaker's hearse.

When young, Lillian planned to go on the stage, having gained a wide reputation as a dancer in amateur theatricals all over Alaska—"from Juneau to Nome!" she told me, laughing. (She was, I'm told, a perfect picture of the old song "Five-foot-two and eyes of blue," and those who saw her dance the Charleston or the Blackbottom always added the song's second line, "but oh, what those five feet can do!") Then she met and married the famed bush pilot "tall, dark, and handsome" Joe Crosson, and soon there were children to care for, as well as further adventuring with her flying husband. In 1949 she lost Joe to a heart attack. Some fifteen years after that she married Scott Frizell, an old friend of Joe's. My thanks to Lillian's daughter, Susan Fraser of Camano Island, Washington State, for arranging my talk with her mother.

Added Note
Clair Okpeaha's run
(see page 61)

The distance of the original run, from the crash site northerly along the coast to Barrow, has been measured at just under twelve miles, but to the Brower house at the north end of the village, not the Daugherty place. Okpeaha was then thirty-nine, and was dressed in a fur parka and heavy boots, and his course included, besides sandy shore, some rough tundra and pooled ocean water. Under those conditions his estimated time for the run of about two hours was quite good, averaging ten minutes per mile.

In August 2008, to mark the fiftieth anniversary of Barrow's incorporation, on the fifteenth, the day of the crash, the Okpeaha Memorial Run was held, retracing his original course. There were some thirty runners, half of them Eskimo, and the weather was brisk and sunny. Runners were lightly dressed: sweat pants and T-shirt with a light jacket. The winner was Hiroki Ikawa, age twenty-seven, a Japanese scientist working in Barrow. His time was two hours and fifteen minutes. The women's winner, in a time of two hours and thirty minutes, was Jeanette Montour of Springboro, Ohio. Along the way three polar bears were sighted, two in the water offshore and one on the tundra within fifty yards of the runners. Men with shotguns and rifles stood guard along the course. A bowhead whale surfaced nearby, as if to watch the race.

SELECTED BIBLIOGRAPHY

Lists books, periodicals, and miscellaneous items, including works read only for background and stimulus. Regular newspaper sources cited in the text and notes are not repeated here.

Alaska and Yukon, A Guide. New York/Chicago: Rand McNally, 1927.

Alaska History. "Modern Tradition: Barrow's Inupiat Adapt Old Ways to 21st Century Tradition." Spring 1995.

Beatty, Jerome. *Will Rogers*. New York: Saalfield, 1935.

Bogart, Humphrey. Unpublished interview by Bill Blowitz regarding Bogart's role in telling Mrs. Rogers and Mary of WR death, Hollywood, 1952. Original notes at Ellis Library, University of Missouri, Croy Papers.

Brower, Charles. Unpublished diary. Original at Rasmuson Library, University of Alaska Fairbanks.

———. Letter to Bert Bernet, December 27, 1935, concerning the crash and the recovery of the bodies. Original at Claremore. Quoted in Collins, *Crash*, 34–35.

———. *Fifty Years Below Zero: A Lifetime of Adventure in the Far North*. New York: Dodd, Mead, 1948.

Brown, W. R. *Imagemaker: Will Rogers and the American Dream*. Columbia: University of Missouri Press, 1970.

Burke, Bob. *From Oklahoma to Eternity: The Life of Wiley Post and the* Winnie Mae. Oklahoma City: Oklahoma Heritage Press, 1998.

Collins, Reba. *Will Rogers and Wiley Post in Alaska: The Crash Heard Round the World.* Claremore, Okla.: Will Rogers Heritage Press, 1984. (Mostly a reprint of original documents, news clips, photos, etc.)

———. "Will Rogers' Daughter Mary" (obituary article), *Oologah Lake Leader.* January 4, 1990, written by a close friend.

Croy, Homer. *Our Will Rogers.* Boston: Little, Brown, 1953.

Daugherty, Frank. (Account by a participant of the recovery of the bodies, a United Press release.) See *New York Herald-Tribune* and *New York World-Telegram*, August 17, 1935, and other papers using the UPI.

Davis, Owen. *My First Fifty Years in the Theater.* Boston: Walter H. Baker, 1950.

Day, Donald. *Will Rogers: A Biography.* New York: David McKay, 1962.

Greist, Henry. *Seventeen Years with the Eskimo.* Unpublished autobiography. At Rasmuson Library, University of Alaska Fairbanks, 1961.

———. *The Northern Cross* (substantial Barrow newsletter, issued sporadically 1929–35). See issue of November 1935 for the crash story. Copies at Dartmouth College Library and Rasmuson Library, University of Alaska Fairbanks.

———. (Recollections of the crash, recovery, and preparation of bodies.) In Croy, 299–305.

Greist, Mollie. *Nursing Under the North Star.* n.p., 1968.

Keith, Ronald. *Bush Pilot with a Briefcase.* New York: Doubleday, 1972.

Ketchum, Richard. *Will Rogers, His Life and Times.* New York: American Heritage, 1973.

Kidder, Lyn. *Barrow, Alaska from A to Z.* Anchorage: Bonaparte Books, 1995.

Lavrakas, Dimitra. "Sad Day at Walakpa," *We Alaskans.* July 23, 1995.

Lindbergh, Anne Morrow. *North to the Orient.* New York: Harcourt, 1935.

Marshall, Robert. *Arctic Village.* New York: Smith and Haas, 1933: reprinted 1991 by University of Alaska Press.

Milton, Joyce. *Loss of Eden: A Biography of Charles and Anne Lindbergh.* New York: HarperCollins, 1993.

Montgomery, E. R. *Will Rogers, Cowboy Philosopher.* Champaign, Ill.: Garrard, 1970.

Morgan, Sgt. Stanley. (Lengthy telegraphed account of crash and recovery of the bodies by a participant.) Quoted in Collins, *Crash*, 32, also in many newspapers of August 17–19, 1935.

Oblak, John. *Bringing Broadway to Maine: The History of Lakewood.* n.p., 1971.

O'Brien, P. J. *Will Rogers: Ambassador of Good Will, Prince of Wit and Wisdom.* Philadelphia: John C. Winston, 1935.

Page, Dorothy. *Polar Pilot: The Carl Ben Eielson Story*. Moorhead, Minn.: Vero Media, 1992.

Post, Wiley, and Harold Gatty. *Around the World in 8 Days: The Flight of the Winnie Mae*. New York: Rand McNally, 1931.

Robinson, Ray. *American Original: A Life of Will Rogers*. New York: Oxford University Press, 1996.

Rogers, Betty. *Will Rogers: His Wife's Story*. Indianapolis: Bobbs Merrill, 1941.

Rogers, Will. *The Papers of Will Rogers*. Vol. 4. Steven K. Gragert, M. Jane Johansson, eds. Norman:University of Oklahoma Press, 2005.

Sterling, Bryan B., and Frances N. Sterling. *Will Rogers in Hollywood*. New York: Crown, 1984.

———. *Will Rogers and Wiley Post: Death at Barrow*. New York: M. Evans, 1993.

———. *Forgotten Eagle: Wiley Post, America's Heroic Aviation Pioneer*. New York: Carroll and Graf, 2001. (Focuses on Post and his career, but uses much material almost verbatim from the 1993 book *Death at Barrow*, 181–354.)

Stone, Fred. *Rolling Stone*. New York: Whittlesey House, 1945.

Tordoff, Dirk. Review of *Death at Barrow*, by Sterling and Sterling, *Alaska History*. Spring 1995.

———. *Mercy Pilot: The Joe Crosson Story*. Kenmore, Wash.: Epicenter, 2002.

Wead, Frank. *Ceiling Zero, A Play in Three Acts*. New York: Samuel French, 1935.

Whitefield, Paul. *The Rough Guide to Alaska*. New York/London: Rough Guides, 2001.

Wynn, Keenan. *Ed Wynn's Son*. New York: Doubleday, 1959.

Yagoda, Ben. *Will Rogers: A Biography*. New York: Alfred A. Knopf, 1993.

ACKNOWLEDGMENTS

⊢∗ ⊨♦⊒ ∗⊣

IF A SMALL ARMY OF ABLE journalists and writers long ago hadn't busied themselves over the Will Rogers phenomenon, the present book could not have been written or at least would have been far less complete and poorer in detail. So to those conscientious newsmen and authors of seventy and more years ago I humbly offer sincerest gratitude. A good share of my thanks, also of course, is hereby tendered to the many more recent writers. For all of them, way back then and now, my notes and the bibliography record my debt.

More specifically I thank the helpful staff of several accommodating libraries: Memorial Library, University of Wisconsin, Madison; the Wisconsin State Historical Library, Madison; Will Rogers Museum and Library, Claremore, Oklahoma, in particular its director, Steve Gragert; the Bangor (Maine) Public Library; Portland (Maine) Public Library; Skowhegan (Maine) Public Library; Rasmuson Library, University of Alaska Fairbanks (Caroline Atuk-Derrick, Rose Speranza, Robyn Russell, and Paul Adasiak); Archives of the Presbyterian Historical Society, Philadelphia; Dartmouth College Library; Ellis Library, University of Missouri at Columbia (John Konzal); the Monroe, Wisconsin, Public Library (Barbara Brewer, director, and librarians Anne Mueller, Linda Bourquin, Maggie Guralski, Rita Grinnell, Donna Oxenreider, and Nancy Myers). Also, for ready and cheerful assistance on Clair Okpeaha and his background: Edith Nageak, the Inupiat Heritage Center of Barrow, and two of Okpeaha's grandchildren, Ida

Okpeaha and Clifford Okpeaha (a member of the Barrow Search and Rescue team), both of Barrow. Thanks to Michael Stotts, mayor of Barrow (a grandson of Charles Brower) and Lollie Hopson, administrator of the Presbyterian Church in Barrow. Also thanks to Marti Sumner, *Fairbanks Daily News-Miner*.

The cheerfully efficient staff at the University of Alaska Press: Robert Mandel, director, and editors Sue Mitchell and Elisabeth Dabney.

INDEX

           ⋈⬧⋊

(Since the Notes & Sources section is linked page by page to the main text, its leading items only are listed here.)